THE STREETS OF

DURANGO

Go ye into all the world, and preach the
Gospel to every creature. . . When
They went from one nation to another,
From one kingdom to another people;
He suffered no man to do them wrong:
Yea, He reproved kings for their sakes;
Saying, Touch not mine anointed, and do
My prophets no harm.
Mark 16:15 & Psalm 105:13-15

Written by:
Roberto Sherman G.

The Streets of Durango

Scripture quotations are taken from the King James Version of the Bible.

Published by New Tongues of Fire Mission Publishing Co.
roberto@duo-county.com

Photograph on the front cover is Roberto Sherman G. on the streets of Durango, Mexico in October 1972. Photograph on the rear cover is Roberto Sherman G. in his cell at the Durango State Prison (CERESO), in January 1976.

ISBN 1-931600-14-7

Foreword

This is a true story. I have gone to lengths to portray the events exactly as they happened. To the best of my knowledge, everything has been expressed with no variance from the truth.

Some events I did not write about. I felt they added no value to the story. Some things I suspected but had no supporting evidence. Rather than speculate, I chose to leave these out of my story. I have waited some twenty-two years before putting the experience in print. Time has not dimmed my memory. The writing may not be first class, but the story ranks with the best.

"Streets" was written to tell my story of three years and six months as a missionary for Jesus Christ, the Lord of the Universe, in Durango, Mexico from October 1972 to April 1976.

The story as written in the following pages is divisive, and could be considered radical; but the most radical and divisive man to ever walk the face of the earth was the Lord Jesus Christ. My feet can in no way fill His shoes, but they do follow His steps.

I well expect the contents of this book to be attacked, and my person vilified and demeaned. No apology or excuse is offered for my stand against the Roman church. At one place in the book, I mentioned that I repented of my action and efforts, but no apologies came forth.

The entire 3½ years are yet to be brought to a final judgment. Having passed through the courts of Mexico and public opinion, there lies but one more court of judgment—the final Day of Judgment by my Father the Judge, who sent me to Mexico and maintained my safety while I was there. On that day, I shall sit in judgment with Him, judging those involved and their deeds done in the flesh in this life, whether they be good or bad. I have no charge to bring against the trespasses committed against myself. As far as I am concerned, the entire span of days lies in peace.

During the time this story took place, I lost all, and counted the loss but gain. *(Philippians 3:7,8)* When Jesus appears, He brings a sharp sword of division. *(Matthew 10:34)* By telling the story at this time, I have no reason to believe the sword of division has been returned to the scabbard.

The Bible says that God Almighty rebuked kings for the sake of God's anointed, and warned people that they should not touch them, nor do His prophets harm. *(Psalm 105:13-15)* I extend my deep appreciation and thanks to the authorities, the men and women, young and old, of Durango—both Catholic and Christian.

Had I not been the beneficiary of heartfelt prayer from my brothers and sisters in Christ in the

United States, Mexico, and many other nations, I would not have been able to stand. It goes without saying that all the glory and honor and thanks go to our Lord and Savior Jesus Christ. His Spirit alone made the great spiritual victory possible.

May the events of this book give hope to those without hope and faith to those who lack faith. May it be a door and a light to freedom for those whose souls are in bondage. No matter who or where you are, your freedom is the light and strength of Jesus Christ in your soul. *(John 8:12)* No one can take this away.

DEDICATION

I thank the Lord Jesus Christ
that He placed me at the feet
of Brother Homer Richard Hall
and his ministry.

Roberto

Thanks

On a number of occasions I have attempted to list the people who have helped me, in one way or the other, to get my story written and published. Each time I found it a nearly impossible task. So many brothers and sisters in Christ have helped me to the point of publishing my story, that there is not room enough to mention them all. I would surely omit someone and later feel remiss for the error.

I am in debt; debt to the body of Jesus Christ for all the spiritual and physical help given to enable me to complete "Streets". I do say "Thank you" to all those who have helped me.

Beyond my thanks, I also say, "Such as I have I give unto thee—in the name of Jesus may your life be blessed."

-Roberto de Durango

A Footnote of Thanks:

I thank God for my enemies. Their hard, harsh, and unjust affliction drove me to my knees as never before in my life. . . . and there, sir, I grew strong in the Spirit of my Father, the Lord Jesus Christ.

Prologue

The foreknowledge of God expressed to me gave me strength and held me when I was in tight spots. Prophecy is an awesome thing. The Almighty Spirit, the Father of all spirits, knows all that has happened and all that will happen. *(Isaiah 42:9)*

There were times when Jesus spoke to me in an audible voice. At times, I would also receive true prophecy through the mail or from one having the gift of prophecy.

I knew men of God who would take the written word of God and with a simple faith, endure through very trying circumstances. My faith, not being strong, was greatly strengthened through prophecy by the Spirit and the written word of God.

There would be times when Jesus did not speak to me; nor did I have my Bible or receive any prophecies. During those times, I would hold on tight to the Christian hope that the apostle Paul wrote of in his letter to the Romans—*"And we know that all things work together for the good to them that love God, to them who are the called according to His purpose." Romans 8:28* I did have a love for Jesus, and I did make mistakes. But through it all, it would work to the good.

Jesus had given me a gift of prophetic discernment. There were times when He would also visit me with prophecy. *(1 Corinthians 12:10)* These were valuable tools in my ministry.

The messenger prophets in the Old Testament were impossible and frightening characters. They were the strength of the small nation of Israel. By their word kingdoms rose and fell. I thank the Lord Jesus for the prophetic knowledge given to me while in Mexico. It greatly strengthened my faith.

I believe there are true prophets today, not just one with a gift of prophecy. The Bible tells us there will come a true messenger prophet after the manner of Elijah before Jesus comes back. The ministry of this prophet will turn the hearts of the children to the fathers. *(Malachi 4:6)* Some say he has already come, and others say he is yet to come. I have heard at least half a dozen ministers say that they were the end time prophet. I think theirs is a mistaken claim; or at least five of them are in error. No doubt it will take the Day of Judgment to reveal this man. *(Malachi 4:5,6; Revelation 10)*

The Lord will not place two messenger prophets on earth at the one time, except the two end time prophet messengers of Revelation 11. Scripture speaks of two who will stand up for a remnant of the nation of Israel at the end times, working signs and wonders after the manner of the Old Testament prophets, during the days when the Spirit of Jesus revisits Israel after the time of the Gentiles. *(Revelation 11)*

The Prophecy

The large canvas tent shuddered and swayed slightly. A good three or four inches of sawdust covered the area around the wide platform from which the visiting evangelist spoke. Movies, TV, radio, and print have all had their day in an effort to discredit the Holy Ghost tent evangelist.

The tall, slender man of God holding forth on the warm southern night wasn't one to be trifled with. He was a true, anointed man of God and had packed tents across the United States and foreign nations for over a quarter of a century.

Sherman stood at one side of the platform with a group of men and women, waiting to see if Jesus would speak through the man of God by a Word of Knowledge or Prophecy. *(Numbers 12:6)* It was very real, and the Spirit of the Great God Almighty was present to right the wrongs that evil had inflicted upon His people. Only the Spirit of Jesus Christ could do this.

The man of God turned and pointed to Sherman. Under the inspiration of the Spirit of God, he said, "Son, it looks bad. I don't see how you will get out of a problem you will face in Mexico, but you will, and I see you telling us all about it when you return." Later, the same man of God gave Sherman three other prophecies concerning his stay in Mexico. Over the coming months, they would all come to pass.

Table of Contents

And through a window in a basket was I let down by the wall, and escaped his hands...
2 Corinthians 11:33

Epilogue
About the author

Chapter One

Paco

But God is faithful, who will not suffer you to be tempted above that which ye are able; but will with the temptation also make a way of escape, that ye may be able to bear it.
1 Corinthians 10:13

Sunday, visitors poured into the prison by the hundreds; mothers, fathers, brothers, sisters, children, girlfriends, or friends who cared to visit one of the inmates at the Durango CERESO (the State-Federal Prison). It was a day of fiesta, a holiday, and a visit from loved ones. The prison flooded with the pastors and priests from the various churches in Durango. The prison baseball team was hard at work against a team from the city. The large visitors' area in the center of the prison compound blossomed into a small village, with blankets serving as tents. Across the prison in their Sunday's finest clothes, inmates waited to be called to the visitors' area. The depression and hostility of weekdays gave way to the anticipation of seeing loved ones.

The Segregation Section housed the men who were considered very dangerous. It was an area of tight security. I had departed from this section about a week before this fated Sunday. The prison officials had decided I was at risk of being harmed.

A number of extremely violent gang members had been placed here. The tension within this section, a two-story white brick dormitory surrounded by 25-foot-high walls with a 35-foot tower on one end, ran high.

Mexico was very merciful in its spirit toward the unfortunate men who found their way into the prison system. The funds allocated to the prison were meager, but the officials did the best they could. By and large there was much freedom in the main prison, but today a small group of men was squatting on the tile floor of the second story shower room sharing joints of marijuana. No one visited these men. They were the off scouring of humanity, men who killed for the joy of seeing blood flow and enjoyed snatching the spiritual life of another to enhance their own spirit. Like a den of coiled rattlesnakes, they inhaled deeply from small cigarettes of marijuana and held the smoke as long as possible. This was their day of happiness. They grinned at each other and entered into another spiritual world to escape the harshness of their present state. If this group had a leader, it was a man named Paco. Paco had honed his fighting skills on the darkest streets in Mexico. He looked like and conducted himself with the pride and assurance of a Mafia Don. Respect and fear swirled around and moved before him.

Touches of gray flecked his sideburns; his dark eyes shifted quickly from side to side and then

ahead with a constant alertness. Anyone who came
within striking range got an in-depth reading—
friend or foe, to trust or not to trust. Paco was a
true killer, and in the jungle we lived in he was
well able to care for himself. He ruled as the high
priest of this dark communion.

Most of the guards were scattered around the
visitors' area to handle the large influx of visitors.
Only Sgt. Parales was on duty, and he stayed in his
small cell one floor below.

From the second story row of windows running
along the hall on the prison side of the dormitory,
you could see across the wall, which separated the
segregation section from the main prison. From
time to time men would shout to each other from
the windows across this wall. Carolina made his
way up the stairs to the second floor.

He could yell to men across the wall and get
news of goings on beyond the prison wall. It was a
beautiful Sunday morning. Popular music blared
forth from the loud speakers placed around the
prison. Anticipation of a moment's escape bubbled
in the eyes of everyone—everyone, that is, except
"Paco" and his gang. For them, it was a pressure
box. The depths of Hell pressed them against the
restraints of law and order they found themselves
trapped in. Their emotions floated on a quick
trigger pin.

Carolina, a tough spirited, muscular, young man
of about six feet, his brown hair slicked back and

dressed in his best clothing, was prepared and waiting for the announcement that his visitor had arrived. He walked down the second story hall looking for someone across the wall he could talk with.

Seeing someone he knew, Carolina made a fatal mistake; he leaned out the window and yelled. Several feet away, Paco was jerked from the darkness by the noise. Carolina had stirred the den of serpents.

Bad blood boiled between Paco and Carolina; for several weeks both had breathed and muttered threats at each other. Paco, his eyes narrowed, his hand on his spike, uncoiled, took several swift strides, and plunged his spike into Carolina's back.

In shock and terror, Carolina turned and with his fists fought a good fight, though mortally wounded. Again and again Paco's spike flashed into Carolina. Blood flowed like crimson fountains as Carolina staggered down the hall and stairs. Gasping and staggering, he found a final resting place in the dust of the small segregation yard. Carolina was dead.

The prison alarm rang and rang as a squad of guards poured into the segregation section. Giving no resistance, but protesting that he was attacked by Carolina, Paco was locked in his cell. After all, he did not start the fight, and all his friends nodded in agreement. Prison is a dangerous place, a man has to defend himself. "I had no other choice," he muttered. "I was attacked by that crazy Carolina!"

It was Sunday, and I stayed in on Sunday and prayed. The halls of my new dormitory were empty, as most everyone was either visiting, at church, or at the ballgame. Pecas, a young Mexican who had recently been saved in the prison, came to my cell and announced that Carolina was "no more."

"No more?" I questioned.

"Yes, Paco just killed Carolina." Pecas then poured out the sequence of events.

I thought back a few days, and thanked Jesus for moving me. I had no doubt that Satan had set a trap for me in the segregation section. I had faith Jesus would make a way of escape. He did, but what was about to come into my life would require a bit more faith and a closer walk with the Almighty God.

In time, Paco was released from the segregation section. He was placed in a cell next to the guard's office in the dorm where I lived, with the presumption that all would be well and he would be under close watch.

One morning, I passed a group of men standing around Paco as he gloried in the telling of his death struggle with Carolina. I asked Joe, a young American who seemed to know what the gathering was about, "What's with Paco?" He looked at me with wide eyes of fear. "Don't you know?" he said. "Paco has told everyone that he is going to kill a gringo." I didn't know, but later found out that Paco had purposed to kill Joe. Paco was on a roll.

Wow, what a mess things had turned into! All the problems I had to cope with between the Catholic Church, the State Department of the United States in Monterrey, the host of daily ills, to say nothing of the harsh circumstances we lived under—and now we had a mad man among us bent on killing one of the three gringos in the compound where we lived.

I felt I was on the bottom of Paco's gringo list. Paco could feel the presence of the Holy Ghost around me, and up to this point he had been inclined to give me a measure of distance in our relationship. This wasn't true with Joe, and I knew Joe would never stand a chance with Paco in a showdown.

I felt I could bind the devil in Paco if we ever came to a face-off. I decided the only way to stop Paco from killing us one-by-one was to confront him and bind the devil in him. I had been blessed with the Holy Ghost and prepared in my prior ministry with spirits, but without Jesus, such a confrontation would be suicidal.

The confrontation was not long in coming. One night not long after finding out that Joe was Paco's next target, several of the men and I were playing a guitar and singing hymns. The Holy Ghost was moving and, in a way, we were blasting spiritual

broadsides. I stamped my feet, danced and sang—
all this, and only feet from Paco's cell.

I knew better than to turn my back. Seemingly,
the gates of hell flew open and Paco uncoiled.
Swiftly he came at me. "No more dancing, no more
singing," he shouted. Quickly I moved to confront
him. This was a surprise to Paco, as I am sure he
felt we would all melt away and he could return to
his cage without further ado.

Everyone knew Sherman didn't carry a knife.
When hit, he would not hit back in a serious fight,
but they all knew Sherman seemed to fear nothing.
I still remembered that prophecy about returning
safely. Somehow, Jesus would see me through this
situation. "I'll kill you," Paco growled.

We met face to face. Anger and indignation
boiled within me. This man, this crazy man who
had killed Carolina, a friend of mine who had come
to the Lord only days before his death, and had
killed many more people on the streets, was now
purposing once more to add a notch to his knife.

I said, "You ain't gonna kill nobody."

Men working in the hall stopped working and
watched. The men around us moved back along the
walls. No one wanted to be caught in the ring when
these two started swinging. Sgt. Parales was once
again on duty. He watched from the protection of
his office as the face-off developed.

Sgt. Parales was in no hurry to stop the issue.
This was the heavyweight match of the prison with

no holds barred. I felt some believed Sherman and Paco could kill each other and the prison would be better off.

We were face to face and eyeball to eyeball. I felt I should throw all the power of God I had as soon as possible, or all the true prophecy I had received was about to fail. The swiftness with which I confronted Paco took him by surprise, and for a second it set him back. From the depths of my lungs I yelled, "JESUS!" with a great fervency, at the same time making a downward motion with my fist and arm. With this move on my part, Paco unloaded a left upper cut to my right cheek. It had such force that I was lifted from the floor. The devil in Paco didn't bind easy, but I came right back down to the same position and was not thrown off balance. Again I yelled, "JESUS!" and again we were eyeball to eyeball; only, this time, Paco was physically frozen.

I think some spiritual burden was knocked off of my head with the first lick I took from Paco. The power Jesus had given me to bind spirits came through much clearer and more powerful the second time I yelled 'Jesus'. I guess I wasn't 'prayed up' as well as I thought I was.

The devil that drove this poor man was bound. Paco could not move. His eyes reflected terror. Here, as he stood helpless, I thought for a moment that I should do something to enhance the standoff. Perhaps I should go stand behind this helpless killer and laugh at him.

The Lord gave me some good sense about this time, and I decided I would hold the matter where it was. A spiritual hell had boiled over Paco's head as he came toward me. I wanted no part of this hell, and wished at this point that I had stayed clear of Paco and his lust for blood and power.

The furnace doors of Hell had been closed, and the flames quieted. For what seemed like many minutes, we stood staring at each other. At this time, a second seemed like a minute. My anger and indignation came to the forefront. Inwardly shaking with anger, I glared at this man. Neither one of us moved. Then, to my right I heard the clang of metal as Sgt. Parales opened his office door. Paco ran, and everyone saw it.

To avoid talking about the incident, I turned and walked to the other side of the dormitory. I had been in the other hall only a minute or so when Parales, wide-eyed, turned the corner and grabbed me. He said, "He's coming after you again to kill you." And with these words, he pulled me into a small alcove under the stairs to the second floor as Paco turned the corner of the small hallway between the two long cell rows. It seemed Parales was sure Paco was going to kill me, but no one knew old Sherman wasn't going to turn the other cheek this time. I could take it no longer. A spirit of murder had come over me. As Paco approached, his path would bring him within feet of the alcove.

For years I had engaged in sports. I saw no problem with hitting Paco head on, lifting him in the air, and busting his head against the cement floor. I braced myself to lunge as he neared. Sgt. Parales had no hold on me, and I set my foot against the wall in preparation to hit Paco. Then I felt a light wind blow across my face, and I found I could not move. The Bible tells us that Jesus will not subject us to more temptation than we can stand, and He will make a way of escape for us. *(1 Corinthians 10:13)* The light wind I felt was the Holy Ghost making a way of escape by rendering me helpless.

Paco passed without saying anything, and Sgt. Parales, not heeding my protest, locked me in my cell. Days followed, and there was no more mention of the matter. I stayed away from Paco and Paco avoided me. I had no doubt that Paco had been touched by God in a mighty way during the confrontation.

Then a strange thing happened. The young kids who had openly laughed at me, and cursed me, now passed with a respectful nod. A bit confounded, I asked Pacas what was going on. "Well," he said, "Paco told a lot of the kids and men in the prison, 'Sherman is a man of God and Jesus is King.'" With these words, he reached people for Jesus who I would never have been able to reach. There was no doubt that Paco was anointed of God.

Later, Paco had a run in with Santos near the

shops where they worked. Santos wasn't killed, but at long last the prison authorities felt it best to keep Paco under lock and key. Carolina had a younger brother in the prison. He was released to prevent possible vengeance and more bloodshed. I attributed the situation as somewhat akin to the Old Testament offering where one bird is killed and another is released in a field. *(Leviticus 14:4-7)* I gave Carolina's brother my sandals as he left the prison.

Later as I talked to a visiting missionary, who for many months had feared to visit me because of the controversy that surrounded my stay in the prison, a group of guards brought Paco by on the way to a hearing in the main office. Paco was in handcuffs with guards in front and in the rear—a pitiful sight. I told the missionary to pray for this man, as he had helped me greatly in the prison.

At that moment, Paco began a great struggle to light a cigarette with his hands bound. The missionary looked at me with great self-righteousness and replied, "You mean he is a Christian and he smokes!"

I at once attempted to defend Paco. "Well, we have to consider just where Paco has come from in his life—but he's growing in Christ and he's not killing people anymore." The chains and handcuffs saw to that, and then indignation flooded me. This man, this self-righteous coward, a man who could have helped me greatly in the prison, had let a couple of years go by before even saying 'hello'. This Pharisee, I could say no more to him. We parted.

I wondered who would stand taller on the Great Day of Judgment *(2 Corinthians 5:10)*; Paco, who had turned parts of the prison upside-down for Jesus, or the very religiously correct missionary? Perhaps I should go buy Paco a carton of cigarettes. I remembered Lincoln's answer to the critics of General Grant when he was told that Grant had a keg of whiskey in his tent and got drunk every night. "Find out what brand he drinks and I'll send a keg to all of my generals. Grant is the only general I have who will fight!"

Later, after fruit for the Lord Jesus had been clearly borne by Paco, I shuddered inwardly at the thought of my bashing Paco's head into the cement. I would have done my Lord and Savior Jesus Christ no service. How thankful I was for His great Mercy, and Grace! For sure the Spirit of Jesus, my God, is a very present help at all times. *(Matthew 28:20)*

Chapter Two

The Streets of Durango

*Go ye into all the world and preach the gospel
unto every creature... Mark 16:15*

Paco had been locked up good and tight. There were others besides myself who thought this a very good thing.

I sat alone in a patch of stubby grass, a hard thing to find in this very large dusty yard. In this place, a moment of privacy was rare, yet I had found a place where no feet or eyes of a guard would bother me. I was granted a few moments of grace. "Leave the gringo alone, he's had his licks!"

I began to think back to the series of events that had brought me to my patch of grass.

The events had started much like a small ship on a calm sea, with cloudless blue skies and no harm in sight. Slowly the sea had begun to roll, and dark clouds appeared, along with sharp gusts that buffeted me and my small craft. With each hour, the sea became rougher with winds and rain and no harbor in sight. Through it all, my sea anchor was holding, and I was riding the storm with my ship. My anchor was Jesus.

I remembered when we topped the rise on the highway into Durango, and before us in the distance lay the streets and buildings of the city of our destination.

Durango, dry and cool, seated on a large plain around six thousand feet at the base of the eastern slope of the Western Sierra Madres... Pancho Villa would fall back to Durango with security after raids along the United States border. The sign on the highway read, 'Durango—Population 140,000'. White and pastel colored buildings, glittering in the morning sun, greeted us as we rolled into the Mexican city of Durango. Encompassed about by the rocky, towering Sierra Madres, Durango stood as a city fortress. I parked the old Volkswagen van Steve and I had driven from the United States alongside the Central Plaza, La Plaza de Armas. Here in Durango my missionary work would begin, and this was to be the spiritual battleground in the coming days.

The plaza, as large as a football field, with an aging Roman Catholic Church pressing from the north end, surrounded by shops, hotels, and various government offices, was to be the ordained ground of spiritual battle. The roses and flowers wound around the plaza and the large central bandstand in beauty and abundance. Many benches lined all sides of the large park, and even at the early hour in which we arrived, the shoeshine men were hard at work. They were the unofficial caretakers of the area.

Though I was greatly motivated by the burning desire to tell people about Jesus Christ and His ever present helping way, I was also motivated by the fear of God. *(Psalm 34:7)* As my ministry progressed in Mexico, I found that I was being buffeted by intimidating forces, and then by forces of fear and terror. To be sure, I felt these strong forces, but there was the fear of God and the fear of failing in my ministry that shook these distracting spirits from me.

The awesomeness of the Almighty God and His Law surrounded me and left no room for intimidation or fear of man. I was accountable to the Lord Jesus Christ for my actions, and if the law and way of man did not line up with the Law of God, then I would choose the Law and Way of God. In this area I felt I had security, resting on the Great Commission of *"Go ye into all the world and preach the Gospel to every creature"* and the actions and words of Peter and John when they were told that they could not talk about Jesus in Jerusalem. *"We ought to obey God rather than men." (Mark 16:15, Acts 5:29)*

I knew when I stepped to the forefront of Plaza de Armas in Durango that I was violating the laws of Mexico. Sooner or later the showdown would come, and both the laws of Mexico and my faith in God's Word would be tested to the limits.

In the meantime, I feared God's law more than I did the law of Mexico. I had to stand, cry aloud and spare not. As a son of the One True God, I had no other choice. *(Isaiah 58:1)* For sure I believed there was a heaven to gain and a hell to shun. The idea of being lost and going to hell was a very great reality to me. *(Luke 16:23)* The idea of going to be with Jesus was an even greater reality. *(Luke 16:19-22)*

The need to warn the individual of the sure sword of death that would come against his life was the driving force behind my ministry. *(Hebrews 9:27)* Etched in my mind and on my soul was the Old Testament scripture in the book of Ezekiel. *(Ezekiel 3:17-21 & 33:1-19)* Jesus had done away with the Mosaic Law, but the Old Testament still reflected the Mind of God. *"Love thy neighbor as thyself." Matthew 22:39* If I were in error, I would want to be warned. The New Testament covers this point also. Paul said in Romans that we do not make void the law through faith, but that we establish the law. *(Romans 3:31)*

The rules of the New Testament didn't change the mind of God in the Old Testament. If the wicked died in his blood and I had not warned, then his blood would be required at my hands. *(Ezekiel 33:6)*

To this point in the life of my family, we had failed God. My grandfather, who was revered as a saint in my hometown and by his own testimony had never missed a day in church for fifty years, had failed God. The Lord Himself told me this. He had been called to the mission field of another nation, but because of the cares of the world and the pressures to provide for a family, he had neglected to answer the call. Somewhere the Word of God had gone lacking. The ease of Zion created a wall of indifference to the suffering of others. *(Amos 6:1)*

Make no mistake about the mission field and preaching the true gospel. It is rough, but nothing alongside of the idea of going to hell. The chickens were starting to come home to roost in my family. I did know that the Bible says you can bring one in error back to God and redeem many a sin. *(James 5:20)*

The owners of hell's pawnshop were calling for their spiritual due. Both my spiritual family and my natural family were going up for cheap sale on the block of eternity if my ministry could not find a justification and pleasure from the King to back off a harsh judgment.

Facing the problem in the natural seemed impossible, but with Christ all things are possible. *(Mark 9:23)* I knew the problem and I knew what to do to solve the problem. I needed an opportunity, and Jesus had set before me the ordained opportunity in Durango.

At times, when I have mentioned sacrifice to redeem sin, I have had people question me with this remark; "Jesus made the sacrifice." This He did, and what a great one it was, but we are called to walk in His footsteps bearing our own cross in His name, a continued sacrifice for sin.

(Colossians 1:24) The cross and crown go hand-in-hand; with no cross there is no crown.

The idea that social position, wealth, or education counted as one's sacrifice to the Lord had robbed my spiritual and natural family. They had traded a holy birthright for a bowl of porridge. They had pawned the Almighty's talents for the deceitfulness of what the world had to offer. Could they be redeemed? Yes, they could. (James 5:20)

Had Jesus shown me what would be required, very possibly my courage might have failed. I would take one day at a time and trust in the Lord Jesus Christ to get me through the spiritual minefield.

We found a very clean room at a pleasant but low-rate hotel next to the Plaza. We had the Volkswagen van, our few goods, and a small motorcycle. For several days we kept the motorcycle in our room, but it became a tricky task to get the two-wheeler out of the room, down the hallway, and down the stairs to the outside. "Please excuse us—please excuse us"—as we wheeled down the hall under the hard stares from the manager. We then decided we would take turns sleeping in the van with the motorcycle.

We established our church directly across from the central Roman Catholic cathedral, which had stood in monolithic majesty for several hundred years. Silently, she stood and gazed upon all who passed, paying scant attention to those who blessed themselves as a salute to her nearness to God. She sat as a queen and feared no one.

Not having been to a formal school to be a missionary or preacher, I was at a loss as to where to start or what to do. Our Spanish was limited to counting money and asking for gas and food.

We had been blessed with the Holy Ghost and Jesus had blessed us with a number of spiritual gifts, the gift of tongues being one. *(Acts 1:8, 1 Corinthians 12:10)* In times past I had been told that I brought forth messages in Spanish while speaking under the inspiration of the Holy Ghost. Steve had been blessed with the same gift.

We had noticed that several men were working around the Plaza with guitars, singing to the passersby. This would be the way we would preach. We would stand next to the street and sing in tongues. We did this for several weeks. When we were not singing, we stood with sandwich boards, scriptures written front and back, and shook hands and waved to people.

We would select a verse from our Spanish Bibles each day and this was our message. Most of the messages were aimed at the rampant worship of wood and stone, and the message that Jesus was coming soon and to prepare to flee the wrath of God.

The message to prepare for the Second Coming of Jesus Christ was taken with great seriousness. "Is Jesus really coming back?" many asked. The dominant theology of the Catholic world insisted that the Pope of Rome was Christ here on earth. That left room for no other to come back. Jesus for sure was the Son of God, but He passed on to sit in triune majesty with the Father, and besides, the Catholics were so blessed with Mary and hosts of dead saints who carried prayer directly to God the Father. *(1 Timothy 2:5)*

The one and only true Mediator was, by Roman doctrine, removed from His singular Lordship. The singular name of Jesus was reduced in power. Blasphemy had entered in to destroy the only Name by which a person can gain entrance into Heaven. *(Colossians 1:14-19)*

The reported visions of the Virgin Mary by Juan Diego were the basis for the prayer to the virgin in Mexico. I cannot say whether Mary did or didn't appear to the humble Juan Diego. This was not the question. The Lord Jesus Christ was the only One Who could remit sin and was to be called upon in prayer. *(1 Timothy 2:5)* Jesus said that all power in heaven and earth had been given to Him, all power in Heaven and Earth. *(Matthew 28:18)* He then empowered fleshly men with His Spirit to do the things He had done. *(John 14:12)* Jesus was fully God in my mind. To debate and argue the matter was fruitless. *(John 14:9)* It was something that had to be shown to a person by Jesus. The Holy Spirit being the Spirit of Jesus became a spiritual matter that could only be understood by one having the mind of Christ. *(1 Corinthians 2:16)* I preached my message for a person to turn to the Spirit of Jesus, the Spirit of Righteousness and all Truth, and prepare to flee the wrath of God to come.

As the days progressed, we found that the wonderful Mexicans received us with an unusual love. Two teenage girls would appear like angels every morning and bring us fruit. The people of the town received us with an unusual show of hospitality and respect.

Steve and I labored day and night, praying for people, singing in tongues, visiting bars or wherever a door opened. Jesus was with us and signs and wonders were following. *(Mark 16:20)* On several occasions, someone who spoke Spanish and English would tell us of the messages we were singing and remark that we spoke perfect Spanish. *(Acts 2:6-12)* I did not speak in tongues when I received the Holy Ghost. I did receive the mind of Christ in understanding the things of God. *(1 Corinthians 2:12)* Understanding the Bible became as clear as understanding the page of a newspaper right after I received the Holy Ghost.

One group of people told me that I had not received the Spirit of God. They said that evidence of receiving the Holy Ghost was a person speaking in tongues. To this day I question this doctrine. Paul did not speak in tongues when he received the Holy Ghost. *(Acts 9:17-18)* I do not believe the manifestation of a spiritual gift is evidence of the indwelling of God's Spirit. The gifts and calling of God are without repentance. *(Romans 11:29)* Later, after fasting and prayer, I did receive a gift of tongues. *(1 Corinthians 12)*

The room was small. Two beds and a small box for clothes made up the furnishings. The adobe walls were covered on all sides, from the top to the bottom, with pictures jammed close together—pictures, large and small, of movie stars; women in brief attire, and some with no attire. Two young men in their teens lay in a bed nearly naked. The skin on their faces was taut, and a sick blackness surrounded their sunken eyes. Their bodies and limbs were bones covered by a layer of flesh and not much more.

The mother had asked me to come and pray for her two sons. As I entered the room, the many faces of the women in the pictures seemed to laugh and jeer at me. Hell's daughters were roasting their prey. The spiritual darkness could be felt. It had done a crippling work on the two young men.

I told the mother that the pictures were points of contact for the devils on the women, and these devils had crippled her sons. They should come down before prayer. She agreed, and I began lifting the pictures from the walls amid the feeble yells of protest from the young men.

Perhaps I made a mistake; I did not destroy the pictures. I piled them outside the room, said a prayer, and left, feeling that I had done a good job. I explained to the mother about the crippling effects of the points of contact—women's spirits with their devils on the pictures. She agreed. The rank idolatry of the area had brought a double dose of iniquity, and overhead the evil pressed the cauldron of hell closer and closer to God's people. *(Jeremiah 16:18)*

I had attended a revival meeting in Monterrey, Mexico and listened intently as the American evangelist pleaded with God to send His judgments upon Mexico. Perhaps the preacher was in the will of God. I was not sure. I somewhat dismissed the plea from my mind and centered my thoughts on getting to Durango. There were some young men in prison in Durango whose parents had asked me to visit as I continued my missionary work.

I did notice that a spirit of haste pushed us toward Durango after the meeting.

God had answered the preacher's call. In the past I had come to realize that the judgments of God are not necessarily destruction. *(Psalm 19:9)* *"Where sin abounded, grace did much more abound"*, and our Great God is a God of mercy and delights in extending grace and mercy. *(Romans 5:20, Micah 7:18)* I did not find it hard to extend my prayer for mercy and grace to others whom, through no fault of their own, found themselves overcome by supernatural forces.

It was not hard to see myself in the individuals who groped in the darkness, being overcome by sin and running amok in a life without knowledge of the truth of Jesus Christ. "Oh, yes, that's me," or "Yes, I've been where you are. Jesus granted me great mercy and grace, and I have faith He can do so for you." *(Romans 9:22-23)*

Armed with this faith based on the great mercy and grace given me, we were being hastily thrust into an oncoming spiritual battle that would require this great measure of faith and understanding. A double portion of judgment hovered over Mexico and ran to and fro searching and gathering its victims.

In the Bible, in the Book of Jeremiah, the Lord tells what He will do to a nation carried away in idolatry. *"And first I will recompense their iniquity and their sin double." Jeremiah 16:18*

In Durango, the cry of the misguided sheep had also reached God and the Lord had loosed a flood of mercy and grace upon their cries. I was only part of the army of God that now converged on the city sitting nearly a mile in the sky.

Others had their part, but it was my prayer that I do my work and be found worthy. *(Luke 21:36) "For unto whomsoever much is given, of him shall be much required:" Luke 12:48*

Whoever ruled Durango would rule Mexico. If Righteousness were to conquer the streets of

Durango, then Jesus would rule Mexico. I was not aware of all the deep spiritual ramifications at the time. In my simple way it was still one day at a time in Jesus.

Later, I was told that the boys whose pictures I had so boldly tumbled out of their room caused so much trouble that their mother had to have the pictures put back on the walls. I didn't know where I had failed, but on the surface the world was not turning to my preaching.

The Plaza was our field for sowing the Word of God. Not only was the written Word of God being sown, the spiritual Word was moving by acceptance, and an unseen work was being done deep in the souls of people. The Ark of the Covenant had come into town.

We found that the bus stop at the Plaza de Armas was fertile ground for sowing the seeds of salvation. One by one and minute by minute, buses belching black diesel smoke with brakes squealing, would pull along the front of the plaza. They were bound for all the small towns around Durango.

We cut two square-foot pieces of cardboard and, with a marker, printed in Spanish, "May we pray for you that Jesus will save your soul?" We then turned our attention to the windows of the loading buses. From front to rear, we passed the windows with our small signs and asked for a show of hands. At times everyone on the bus would hold up his or her hands, at other times only a few. The work was endless.

It became evident that the forces of hell had been stirred. There were times people would hand us a dollar or two, but each time we handed it back. We had written on our sandwich boards that we would not accept any money. From time to time, strange characters would hang around, watch for long periods of time, and then disappear. Then the spiritual unrest surfaced in an article in the local Catholic newspaper. *"How dare those gringos do what they are doing in our fair city! No Mexican would be received in the United States as these gringos have been and be allowed to preach on the streets as they have done. Wait and see. God's judgment will get those gringos in the plaza."* There it was, the opening shot across the bow of our ship. We had been warned.

About this time, Steve decided he wanted to return to the United States and departed. I felt this was the will of God. Now, it was Jesus and me.

A Mexican Christian insisted that I come and stay with him in his home. This wonderful man had a small mission at his home and in the coming days would suffer for befriending me. I felt there would be trouble. I had heard true stories about what the Catholics did to the Christian missionaries from the United States. As we progressed in the daily spiritual war, I tried to leave and return to the streets. I wanted to cause this godly man no trouble, but was assured there was no problem.

My single stand in the plaza was not uneventful. I was detained by Federal Police and driven to the house of the man who had befriended me. Here, I was questioned in depth about my motives and religion at the persistent prodding of a political agent. The police seemed satisfied—I was no threat to the nation and my papers were in order. This backed my political tormenting friend reluctantly off my case.

I was being probed by the Catholic element, and from all indications they did not have any legal power to harm my work. Nor was their spirit strong enough to turn the Federal authorities.

The fox was on the run. The people of Durango were not a group of spiritual lackeys. The event passed and another hurdle was crossed.

At this point, I started using my motorcycle to visit various small villages around Durango. The Christians warned me that I would be beaten or shot. I insisted that I wouldn't. After much prayer, I cranked the small motorcycle up and headed west. The road gave way to a railroad as I climbed into the mountains. It was a freedom from the dusty streets that I enjoyed. I bounced along the railroad ties and soon ran into a small group of houses. I stopped at a small grocery store and bought a soda. They were stored on a shelf and warm as the day, but wet. A group of young men gathered around the motorcycle. They were tough dudes and I was a gringo. "My oh me!"

The streets of Durango seemed very safe at this moment. They wanted to ride the motorcycle. I feared that if they did get on the cycle, even if it was recovered, the cycle would be in no shape to get back to Durango. One thing for sure, my God and very present help was with me. The Lord spoke to my mind and said, "Take them for a ride." I motioned for the largest of the men to get on the rear seat. I cranked the cycle and away we went, up and down the dry creeks and washes. I gunned the bike, twisted, and turned with the big fellow hanging on for dear life. I returned to the village, stopped, and announced, "Next?" The big guy dismounted in mild shock and white in the face.

Again, the motorcycle rocked and rolled its way through the bush. I returned with another rider in mild shock, and before it was over, half the village got to ride. I was the circus come to town. I then told them a short message about Jesus and handed out prayer cloths. All in high spirits, they pointed me the way back to Durango. The Bible does say, *"He that receiveth whomsoever I send receiveth me; and he that receiveth me receiveth him who sent me."* There is a lot to be said in receiving a man of God, or in giving him a cool drink of water. *(John 13:20, Matthew 10:40-42, Mark 9:41)*

I had purposed to visit one village to the south of Durango. Again, I received wide-eyed warnings that the Catholics would shoot me at this particular village. I arrived fully expecting the shooting to break out. I had been warned by Jesus that it was part of my ministry to go to this village, warn and pray for people. By doing so, I would be able to keep a harsh judgment from coming upon my family. *(James 5:20)*

I was greatly received by the young people. I had parked my van with messages of the soon coming of Jesus painted on all sides in Spanish, at the small village plaza. I handed out prayer cloths to anyone who would take one, and no one refused. *(Acts 19:12)* The kids thought the van and the prayer cloths with Jesus printed on them were "cool".

Very few men were present, and the women and children dominated the small plaza where I parked my van. Most of the men had gone to the United States to work. The village had gathered for a funeral. The small Catholic Church was filled up with the few men and women of the village. A large crowd of young people sat and milled around the plaza where the old van silently blared out the soon coming of Jesus. The kindness and love of the children and their questions about Jesus touched my heart deeply, and it was there in the village of Nayar that I fell in love with the people of Mexico. I departed from the village with a deep conviction of the truth of my ministry.

It was not my intention or purpose, nor had it ever been, nor is it today, to overthrow the powers that be in a government or church. I held a respect for God because He ordained the powers that be. *(Romans 13:1,2)* The Roman Catholic Church was for a purpose and would survive until that ordained time when Jesus chose to end it.

It was my intention, however, to warn the ungodly and those in error to change. Concerning the Roman Catholic Church, it was my purpose to encourage those within its walls to come away from the bondage of false religion and the wrath of God that followed false teaching, and turn to the Truth. *(John 14:6)*

Spain had come and gone, the French had seen their day pass in Mexico, yet Rome had endured. Very few people understood that the Roman Catholic Church was only part of the nation of Rome, a nation bent on world domination using all the intrigue and lying power of Satan. The nation of Rome ruled Mexico with a spiritual bondage of statues, candles, robes, fear and promises, threats and lies. How the soul of Mexico cried out, "Jesus yes, Rome no!"

Satan and Rome are not to be overthrown until that ordained time, but the spiritual freedom of a person can be found in a moment by turning to the truth of Jesus Christ. The spiritual freedom of Mexico could be found by the people of that nation turning to the Spirit of Jesus.

I returned to the plaza and my stand for Jesus with newfound love for Mexico, coupled with the ever-present fear of God. The motorcycle became my means of transportation. I parked the van and took to the streets of Durango on the cycle.

On occasions, I would dodge oranges and rocks that sailed at me as, head down, I rushed through the narrow streets towards the center of town. I am not sure that I waxed so very bold, or that I increased in stubbornness, but I made an even bolder stand at the Plaza.

It was at this time that I was asked to see the mayor of the town. In a very polite, but firm manner I was told the mayor wanted to see me. "Be there at 11:00."

Entering the office of the mayor the next morning, I wasn't sure just what was about to transpire, but I was sure that I was not going to be awarded keys to the city. The mayor was out, so I talked to the assistant mayor. He informed me that I was breaking the law of Mexico by standing in the Plaza. He then pointed to the article in the national constitution that prohibited such, "No religion in the streets." He was very polite, but I must no longer break the law and should leave town at once. He offered to pay my way to the next city.

I then agreed I was breaking the law, and in parting I mentioned I would leave the city but perhaps continue my work in the surrounding rural areas outside the city. He became very upset and with gestures of the arms and hands, he repeated, "Belfast, Belfast," a number of times. He then went on to tell me that the situation that existed between Catholics and Christians in Durango was akin to the bloody strife in Northern Ireland between the Catholics and Protestants. He went on to say that a large number of Americans were due to visit Durango in a caravan of trailers and the officials of the city wanted no harm to come to me. Simply put, they didn't want a dead American on their hands as they proclaimed the safety and beauty of their city to the Americans and their dollars to spend.

He finally said, "All right, you may stay in the Plaza." The question as to my violation of the laws of Mexico could be debated. The law forbids religion in the streets and was in fact aimed at the Roman Catholic Church. During the past civil war, the Catholics sided with the losing force. The men who won the war knew the church for what it was and made laws to curb it, but they did not do away with her.

A few nights later, as I stood at my lonely pulpit, I heard a noise come from the street at the other end of the plaza. Up the street came a soft drink truck and a mob of young men carrying torches. The loud speaker blared out that the mayor was going to "run the gringo out of the Plaza." The truck and troop of young men passed in front of me, the kids huffing and puffing with their torches held high. Several small bombs went off around me and then, as quickly as they had come, they left. I never understood the meaning of the demonstration except it be to intimidate both the mayor and myself.

If this was the Catholic high watermark of intimidation, it sure betrayed a weakness, and this caused me to be greatly heartened. They didn't have the grip on the city government they wanted. A great restlessness in the spirit had come upon Durango, and like a giant disturbed in his sleep, Durango was taking measure the cry of fire.

The true people of God were stirring under spiritual conviction, and a general call for a crusade in prayer was heard in many quarters of the city.

The soul of the city was crying out to God.

As I stood in my pulpit one afternoon, a large mob of several hundred students approached the plaza—angry young men, lean and hungry for trouble. In a moment, I found myself surrounded by hundreds of these young men. These fellows were tough, lean, and they meant business. Their rage was to be vented on someone, and what better place was there to start than with the gringo in the plaza?

How the priests at the church must have smirked as they watched the gringo engulfed by the raging mob. He had been warned, and now the judgments of God were upon him.

Chapter Three

The Judgments of God

*As for the head of those that compass me about, let the
mischief of their own lips cover them. Psalm 140:9*

Brown, angry faces pressed against the gringo
with the foolish sandwich boards. Some voices
demanded money; others berated him for the
slaughter in Vietnam. (The war in Vietnam was at
its peak.) I faced hard, demanding young men,
venting their hostility on the American standing in
their way. "What next?" I thought. Unless Jesus
came upon the scene, I was about to be torn limb
from limb by a raging street mob. I had been given
true prophecy; this mob confrontation would occur,
and I would come out of it unharmed. Now, here I
was faced with the reality of the prophecy. "Jesus,
don't let it fail!" was my heartfelt prayer. I was
being pressed and pushed about when I called upon
my Father and His ever-present help. *(Romans 10:13)*

"Jesus!" I shouted as loud as I could. *Would
He help me?* At that moment, what seemed like a
blanket of electricity fell upon the mob. Jolts of
God's Holy Spirit flew with lightning speed over
the brown faces, stunning them. Confusion and
fear took hold of all present. I, too, was startled
and in awe of what Jesus was doing. The mob
melted away like ice cream on a summer day. In

shock, they backed off.

How my heart went out to these young men. I had to chase the leader half a block to be able to talk with her. The leader of the group was an older woman. The dramatic demonstration of power by the Holy Ghost had greatly frightened her. A Christian I had met on the street came by, and I asked him to help me tell the lady they did not have to use force to obtain what they wanted. They could turn to Jesus, and He would help them. His English was adequate to understand what I said and in turn translate it into Spanish. She nodded as he talked. The jolting experience she had just been through kept her silent.

After a bit, she told us her story. The young men were students at a small rural college north of Durango. They wanted to expand their small college. One man owned all the land around them and would not sell them any of it; they had a problem, but seemingly not so much of a problem as to necessitate a march in the streets of the state capital. As I talked to some of the students milling around the plaza, I became aware there were several men with the students who seemed "out of place."

These men were not students; I was being introduced to the communist missionaries. The picture was coming into focus. The students had made no commitment to communism. They had a love for their nation and law and order, but were being stirred to extremes by the communist agents.

It became apparent that these students might be dealt with harshly, and there could be bloodshed. The communists, no doubt, would have no loss of sleep if some of the students were killed for their (the students') cause. These "outsiders" would then have the martyrs they needed to cause the students to commit themselves to the gentlemen from Russia.

I talked at length with the "agents", but their minds were as fixed on converting the students with their socialist lies as the Catholic priests were with their lies. In turn, they tried to convert me into their way. An invitation to join them and receive a free trip to Russia to see the glories of all their cities was declined.

I know I am pretty much of a dope, but I felt that the free trip to Russia might turn into a free trip six feet under somewhere down the road.

The students set about taking over the plaza like an invading army. Lumber was hauled in, and wooden tents were thrown up in various places in the plaza. Several central fires were started and supper was cooked and served to the small army. Beautiful little Mexican girls from the school did their part to help.

Everyone was so very serious. The entire group had been fasting for five days, and they meant for their demands to be met. They all seemed to love Jesus, and it was only a short time before I was received as one in sympathy with their cause. A long wooden tent overran my pulpit, and the young men took for themselves the attention that had been focused on me.

I was a good person and they loved Jesus and His whole family, but they had to be about the business of letting people know about their problems. I made myself known but kept a distance from the situation. I would show up every night on my motorcycle and find a place to stand with my sandwich boards. The Bible does say that God, by the foolishness of preaching, chose to save them that believe. *(1 Corinthians 1:21)* There couldn't have been anything more foolish than myself standing with sandals, worn out clothes, and sandwich boards as a small Times Square crowd swirled around me.

The beautiful rose bushes and flowers were taking a pitiful beating. The students were stomping them, along with the thick grass, into muddy matting. The students had come to stay for a while, and nightly the campfires blazed as they determined to measure the town for their rights.

One man came by me, stopped, broke out laughing, and said, "The judgments of God are upon the bushes and grass of the plaza."

With much patience, the mayor and the city endured the situation.

The weekend was upon us, and a full piece band took to the large gazebo behind my stand. As the students gave out pamphlets and solicited agreements concerning their grievances, visitors from all over the city converged upon the plaza. It was a fiesta.

I felt secure surrounded by the students. Whatever evil had been purposed against me had taken a rear seat to the small army that now occupied the plaza. If this was God's judgment, then it was all right with me.

The weather was beautiful, a bit cool and very dry. There were no clouds, and the stars looked down upon the plaza with a dazzling clarity. The band behind me broke into several stirring marches and hundreds of people passed before me. My preaching was taking a back seat to the air of the fiesta. More than anything, I watched the parade of events with silent wonder.

Suddenly, right before me a scuffle broke out, which quickly escalated into a one against two street fight; no spikes or knives, but one of the two had a very sharp cement trowel. He took down the single man, and his buddy with the trowel proceeded to stab at the young man who had been thrown to the sidewalk. Someone once told me that you don't get into a knife fight with fists, nor do you go into a gunfight with a knife. These words made a little sense, but if something wasn't done quickly the little man on the sidewalk was about to have his guts spilled out onto the plaza. Good or bad, he needed help. Not wanting to charge into the situation alone (being the gringo, I felt all three might turn on me), I grabbed one of the students beside me and gave him a shove towards the fight. At the same time I yelled for my Dad. "Jesus!" I shouted, and several times more I called on the Mighty King of the Universe. A strange thing happened; a wall of spiritual force appeared between the two men and the young man on the sidewalk, and they bounced back off of it when they tried to reach him. Again they tried, but to no avail. As people started to gather, the two decided they should call it a day and left.

The young man on the ground jumped up and departed also. The young student and his friends all cut their eyes at me, the clown in the plaza. "Something happens every time this guy yells 'Jesus'!" The event did not go unnoticed.

A few minutes later the young man who had been thrown to the sidewalk reappeared. He now had a buddy, and his buddy had a large butcher knife in his right hand. He acted like he wanted to cut up on someone, maybe anyone. He gazed at me, but the young man whom Jesus had protected on the sidewalk quickly stood between us and assured him I had helped him as he lay on the sidewalk. About this time, a small group of children who begged on the street flooded around me. I had bought them all shoes. Slowly, the man with the large knife looked away from me. This made me very happy.

Later, the young man invited me to have drinks with his gang at a restaurant nearby. "No beer," he said to his followers in respect to me, and I bought sodas for all around. We got on the subject of religion, and I told him that you had to get in touch with Jesus as He alone was the way to God. *(1 Timothy 2:5)* This didn't set too well as he pulled his picture of the virgin from his wallet.

I assured him the virgin was a blessed woman and the instrument by which Jesus came into the world, but she had no power to hear our prayers or remit sin, and she also had received the Holy Ghost on the day of Pentecost. *(Acts 1:14)* The theology was just too deep for all. We finished our sodas, and I told them "God bless you" and departed.

Several days later when I arrived at the plaza, the farmers from the area where the students lived had arrived in force. The plaza had become the center of an even larger army and they brought buses. The students announced they were going to stay in the plaza until their demands were met.

The plaza had turned into a mass of trodden down bushes and mud. You could feel the tension between the authorities and the students; I had not seen the communist agents lately. I had heard snatches of conversation that alluded to the fact that some of the young men from the mountains of Durango had indeed been fighting against the

United States in Vietnam. This gave me a funny feeling.

All around the town, the students had knocked on doors and passed out petitions of their demands. This was an all out effort.

That afternoon the farmers blocked off the streets around the center of the town with their buses. Men and students climbed atop the buses and with bullhorns made known their demands. The air crackled with tension as squads of police looked on.

Then the "sit in" was over, and as quickly as they had come the students were gone. I found a remnant of students sitting despondently on one of the plaza benches. I had come to know the leaders of the students and had tried to help them in any way I could. To many of them, I had given motorcycle rides around the town. I asked them what had happened. They told me that the mayor had ordered them out of the plaza and out of the streets. Their demands had not been met. They looked at me, and one of the leaders said, "Perhaps Jesus will help us?" I said, "I sure pray He will."

I never found out if the students obtained the land they had made such an effort for, but thousands had been reached for Jesus. Unknowingly, the students' efforts had yielded a far more valuable Victory than the land.

Chapter Four

The Gates of Hell

Nevertheless, if thou warn the wicked of his way to turn from it; if he do not turn from his way, he shall die in his iniquity; but thou hast delivered thy soul. Ezekiel 33:9
...and the gates of hell shall not prevail... Matthew 16:18

Events after the departure of the students seemed to drag. The efforts of the students on behalf of their demands had dispelled the idea that I was still a target at the plaza. The World Series was over, the seats were all empty, and yet, there I stood. The ordained moment of God had come to an end. What would I do now?

I had reached multiplied thousands of people, and now the revival was over. I took to the mountains near Durango, and there, in waiting, searched my heart for a leading from Jesus.

Perhaps I would go further south in Mexico, or back to the United States. Then Jesus began dealing with me about the priests at the large Roman Catholic Church in Durango and the city of Durango. He made it known to me that He had a special love for the people of Durango, and for some of the priests in the church, but because they were in great danger of losing their souls, He was going to have to destroy the city and many people.

My efforts had not turned the oncoming sickle

of judgment. We had been weighed in the balances and found wanting. Jesus then directed me go to the Roman Catholic Church at the plaza, confront the priests, and warn them. *(Ezekiel 3:19)* By doing so, I would back the judgment from Durango and my own family, who once again seemed to be on the block of judgment.

Great doubts assailed me. Was this knowledge that I had received of God? What was I doing here in Mexico, alone and hundreds of miles from anyone I knew, or trusted to talk with? Loneliness set in on me. Confusion pounded upon my head. The matter was in my hands alone. I decided I would tell no one of what I felt were the orders of the King.

The Mexican family who had befriended me was all smiles upon my return from the mountains. The students had returned to their town north of Durango. Hundreds upon hundreds of people had been reached for Jesus. God's work had been done. It should have been a time of happiness and thanksgiving to Jesus. I knew better and decided I would use the old spiritual cop out—I needed to pray about this. I did set a date and time in my mind and heart when I would go to the church, serve notice, and warn. This was all I could do.

That old friend of mine, the Fear of God, stayed heavy behind me. A number of years before, I had asked a friend of mine whom I considered to be a true man of God to pray for me for a spiritual gift of wisdom. I fancied I needed some wise thoughts to manage my efforts in God's ministry.

Later, I read in the Bible that the beginning of wisdom was the Fear of God. *(Psalm 111:10)* I don't know if I ever got beyond the beginning stage of this gift, but I sure knew the sharpness of the Spirit of the Fear of God. It unsettled all my fears and doubts. The wise thing to do was to follow the orders of the Almighty, come the gates of hell or high water.

The date I had set in my mind arrived. I saddled up the small cycle and rode to the plaza. I parked the two-wheeler knowing I might not see it again. All my thoughts were left behind and here I was, not sure I would come out alive. My entire life was on the line, or at least I felt this way.

I had prepared a poster with the warning to the priests. I took a hammer and a few nails to nail the warning to the door of the cathedral. I reached the door and begin tacking the 2x4-foot warning poster to the church door. It was early morning and the few passersby paid little attention to the lone man hammering on the church doors.

"Bam, bam, bam." The hammering echoed through the aged building. Hell's cage was being rattled! I placed the hammer aside and entered the church, shouting in tongues. *(1 Corinthians 12:10)* A priest led a group of men from the rear of the church toward me. As I started down the long aisle, I was met with a profusion of idols and statues. My hand went up as I passed a three-foot wooden statue of a woman. My hand hit the doll a glancing blow, and with a big "blam" she hit the floor.

About this time, a group of men, led by the priest in charge, met me at the center of the building. Oh, brother! Hate for my presence and invasion of their holy ground glistened in their eyes. I was going strong with my preaching in tongues as the confrontation merged. *(Acts 2:4)* As we came within several feet of each other, the priest unloaded a black belt punch to the lower part of my chin. A hand from somewhere lifted my head and the strike touched nothing. It went just under my jaw and did not extend as far as my throat.

The priest withdrew a pace and made chopping motions with his hands. I thought, "Hey, this fellow knows what he's doing." Then with a quick run he unloosed a flying kick to my groin. He missed again. The Spirit of God was resting upon me so strong that he bounced backward. I gave him a helping hand, all the while keeping up my preaching in tongues.

The priest yelled for everyone to get back, they had a raging madman on their hands. Later, I was to learn that the priest was a judo expert. He told the newspapers that he had thrown everything he knew in an effort to bring me down, and nothing would work.   I thought it a bit unkind to be attacked in a church. *(Mark 13:9)* Thank God, Jesus was with me again.   I began to feel much better about my actions.

The cathedral confrontation became a standoff, with me yelling in tongues and the priest yelling at me in English, saying that I didn't know what I was saying.

About that time, two little policemen dressed in blue arrived.   "Come with me," one said.   I was about to fall, for I was creeping up on my forty-first birthday and the strength of my youth was taking flight.   With no protest on my part I departed the cathedral with the two policemen.

The matter was over.   Had I pleased the Lord Jesus?   These people knew not what they were doing.   The worship of idols and statues had brought the wrath of God swirling around those that bowed down to wood and stone. *(Deuteronomy 28:15-68)*

The rain did not fall as it should to bring in complete crops and when it did, it came down with such force and measure as to wash away the crops. Disease and pestilence roamed with a free hand. *(Deuteronomy 28:15-68)*

Many Mexicans had learned to live in this cauldron of evil.   Their protection was a fervent charity and an extending love from way down deep in their hearts. *(1 Peter 4:8)* With this, they endured the harshness of a hard land.   They, too, knew my old friend, the Fear of God.

I was escorted to a little blue Volkswagen bug and placed in the front seat. As we pulled away from the church, I watched the priest who had attacked me tear my message of warning from the church door, and then reach over to where I had left the hammer and grab it. He then closed the door with my message and hammer in hand.

The little blue Volkswagen stuttered to the city police station several blocks from the plaza.

Chapter Five

Chilly Christmas

Wherefore the princes were wroth with Jeremiah, and smote him, and put him in prison... Jeremiah 37:15

The two little men in blue escorted me into a large room at the police station. Perhaps a dozen policemen were working at various small desks within this area. One policeman sat at a very high desk overlooking the entire area. Slowly, the place turned into a stew pot of confusion and noise.

The situation dazed and startled me. People were yelling and running, and I could understand nothing. I stood watching the whole matter. Rushing through the door came several men carrying cameras with "Press" written on them. The newspapermen had arrived. "Where is he, where is he?" they shouted. I wondered, "What in the world is going on?"

Someone pointed to me, and flash bulbs from their cameras started popping. Then they were gone. Next came the priest from the cathedral. He talked for a while at the other end of the large room, signed some papers, and departed.

I turned my attention to the two men who had brought me to this point, and one started screaming and turned sideways as he stared at me. He put his hands over his eyes to shield them. The room of about ten policemen looked back and forth between the policeman and myself. He must have seen a blinding light of sorts. Jesus had let such happen before in my ministry as a wonder and sign following.

I didn't know what was going on, but I knew Jesus was surely with me, and these men in blue of Durango were treating me with courtesy. I was placed in a narrow, crowded cell. The cell was the old prison toilet room. It was filled with young men. As soon as the cell door clanged shut, I was confronted by several of them. They were homosexuals. They started making various sucking noises with their mouths and pinching my arms and legs. I kicked the nearest kid and found myself a corner to set my back against a wall. I started kicking and punching as the mini-mob came at me. In another minute or so, I was going to hit the floor.

From under a large piece of cardboard came a little guy. (The cardboard was his blanket.) He started yelling and the group stopped and backed off. "Stop, stop, stop!" he said. "This is a man of God! Stop!" He had been to a Bible school in Juarez, and though he had no respect for others' property, he did have respect for God and His men. His words backed the men in the cell off with their advances.

I thanked him and gave him my jacket, which had 'Jesus is coming soon' written in large letters, front and rear—in Spanish. I was later to see him again at the state prison outside Durango.

I then looked up and saw a small altar fastened to the wall, with a candle flickering dimly on top. Seeing as how I was going down the tube for preaching, I might as well keep on. This was no time to stop.

I reached up and snuffed the candle out, took the altar down, and told those present that this wasn't the way. It was as if I had triggered a small explosion inside the cell. Such screaming and yelling I had never heard. No one wanted or cared to hear me. It continued unabated for several minutes. The guys in the cell started calling for the police. What a crazy place!

The police came running, pulled me from the cell, and left me standing in the hall. In the next cell were about twenty men. They started screaming also. I didn't know what they were screaming about, but I decided to continue preaching the message of the soon coming of Jesus.

I went to the next cell with the other screaming men and started shaking hands and telling them that Jesus was coming soon. The crescendo increased, and several men started climbing the bars. Even with all the screaming and yelling, everyone seemed to be in good spirits.

The police were in great consternation, and a group of them gathered at the hall entrance to mull the matter over. The next thing I knew the cell door was flung open, and the whole group was turned loose on the streets. Then I was escorted into the large cell and the door was slammed shut.

There I sat in the large empty cell. Then, I began to talk to Jesus. "I knew it, I knew it, I don't know what you told them, but you sure made them mad."

I was talking to Jesus in reference to me speaking in tongues. Perhaps 30 or 40 minutes passed, and I had time to ask Jesus for a few favors. For one, I asked Him to send the greatest men of God in the land through the doors of this jail. Over the many months to follow, they came through the cells of the police station on the way to the prison, beaten, dirty, and condemned.

After a short period of time, the man who had befriended me and let me stay in his home was brought in and placed in the large cell with me. He looked at me in silence, then smiled and said, "How many did you shove over?" I assured him I did not go to the cathedral with the intention of shoving over statues. I went there to warn the priest.

He told me the police had come to his house, arrested him, and taken my Volkswagen van. The matter was escalating. I never thought my actions would have incited such a fervor.

A few minutes passed, then several policemen appeared and told me to come with them. We walked to an office across the street. I was brought to the office of a man whom I was told was a judge. As I waited, his secretary gave me a soda. This act of kindness made my day.

I was then brought before the man of the office and told that I would be placed in the state prison as soon as possible that day. The normal time for a person to travel through the paper work from the jail downtown to the prison was ten days. Everyone seemed to want me off their hands. I think I could have very easily walked off that day and left Durango. No handcuffs were put on me, and at times I was left to myself. As I left the judge's office, I asked him if I might pray that Jesus would save his soul. "Oh, yes!" he replied. Several weeks later, he was placed in a room next to mine. (This was in the clinic at the state prison.) The prayer reached Jesus. Over the weeks to follow, we became good friends.

Before leaving, a group of men came into the room. One asked me who I was. I said, "A son of God." They all laughed. "He says he is Jesus." "No, not The Son of God, but a son of God," I replied. The matter went over their heads. *(John 1:12)*

From the judge's office, I was taken to the state prison outside of Durango. Here, I was taken to the segregation section and locked in a 10×6 foot cell. I didn't know what was coming next. No one told me anything, except to say, *"Go there,"* or *"Come here."*

When I was placed in the bare cell at the state

prison, I felt like a piece of meat no one wanted, wrapped up and put in the freezcr.

Christmas was a day or two away, and the small cell had no heat, nor did the building. High in the mountains, Durango was often visited by snow this time of year. It was cold. I had only a T-shirt and a thin pair of pants. Somewhere along the way I had lost my sandals. I felt I might as well have been on the moon. I didn't see anyone for a number of hours. Then, the men who brought the evening meal came by with their beans in water buckets and small loaves of bread. I didn't have anything to eat with, and I really wasn't too hungry. They passed on by.

Night came, and still no authorities, no papers, no nothing. The cell was bare except for a small toilet and water basin. The entire hall was vacant. The upside of the situation was that the place was very clean, and I was protected from whatever chain of events had spawned in Durango.

I asked a passing guard if I could have a blanket. He said, O.K., he would send me one, but it never came. Even as cold as it was (the temperature must have been near freezing outside), I wasn't cold. There was no heat in the building.

It was then that a great love and happiness filled my soul. Even though I was in the inner prison, I was free in my soul and happy. I began to sing, "Thank you Jesus for making me Your son." I sang and sang. The events of the day had exhausted me, and I felt very far from friends and country, but so close to Jesus. I curled up on the cement floor and went to sleep in a great peace.

The treatment I received was not unusual. There were so many people, and very few guards to take care of the place. People entered the front door, and then they had to fend for themselves.

Charity among the inmates abounded. There were four Americans in the prison on drug charges. I had visited them several times, so it was a great surprise when they found I was in the segregation section. They were able to find a couple of blankets, a plate, a cup, and a spoon and get them over from the main prison to me.

The Mexican legal system was a hand-me-down from the French rule of Mexico, and the Napoleonic code of law. If indicted, you were guilty until proven innocent with an added twist; Americans were not given bonds of release.

I did not know what was going on outside the walls of the prison, but it seemed that a monumental effort was under way to tell the world of the great crime that had taken place in Durango.

The presses of vilification were working overtime. The tide of the Catholic media swelled toward the national conscience. Newspaper, radio, and TV in Mexico spoke, often with bold headlines, of my crime.

The honor and dignity of Mexico was on the line, or so the Catholic press wanted to portray the

event. The bare-footed, drug-crazed, gringo hippie
had violated the holiness of the cathedral, swinging
a hammer, and damaging the sacred idols of God.
My actions had become an international 'cause
celèbre'.

I was very thankful for the blankets, eating
utensils, and even a Bible, jacket and shoes.
Things were looking up.

Christmas Eve rolled around, and the guard
unlocked my cell and told me I was free to walk up
and down the hall. I mumbled something and
stayed in my cell.

I felt as if I was in a tub going 'helter-skelter'
through the rapids on a twisting, turning river.
What was to come next? My life was beyond my
control; it was one day at a time, sweet Jesus.

Two men with a camera came to my cell. I was
lying on a small cot and they asked me to stand up.
The authority of their request went by my head.

Then they said they were from NBC or CBS, or
something like that. Of course, I would want my
picture on TV. I felt like throwing something at
them. Nothing was handy. One of the guards
grabbed my Bible and I rose from my cot and
grabbed it. What joy prevailed among the
cameramen! The gringo was stirred into action. I
then pointed my finger at the two men and their
camera and said, "I warn you not to make a
mockery of Jesus Christ or His man." With that,
they were gone. It was Christmas, and I didn't

want to see any more jolly men with their video cameras.

The streets of Durango seemed very far away.

Later, the earthquakes came, and thousands were killed as they shook and rocked the Latin American world from Mexico to deep in South America. Durango was spared. Jesus was true to His Word. The angel of destruction had passed over the city. The blood of sacrifice had been placed on the door. *(Exodus 12:13)* Jesus sure did have a special love for the people of Durango.

Chapter Six

The Clinic

...that they should commit Jeremiah into the court of the prison... thus Jeremiah remained in the court of the prison... Jeremiah 37:21

Life was bearable in my cell. I was alone and protected. The men with the beans and bread came by two or three times a day. Somehow I felt I would be out of prison and on my way back to the States in a few days. It didn't work out that way.

A guard came to my cell and told me I had a telephone call. I felt as if I was at the North Pole and had just received a call from home.

I was escorted to a very modern office, and behind a large desk sat the Director. With an unusual courtesy I was given the telephone and told that the caller on the other end was calling from the United States State Department in Monterrey.

A woman's concerned voice asked me if I was all right, as they had read in the newspaper of my crime. I sure appreciated the call and concern. I told the lady I was all right and that Jesus was with me. She said, "He sure must be." We talked briefly, and she said they would be in contact with me.

I hung the telephone up and was told by the Director that he would do all he could do to help me with my situation. He suggested that I be placed in the clinic, as the treatment in the segregation section was somewhat harsh, but they had to keep it so to deal with the kind of people who were placed there.

The clinic was a small one-story brick building near the main office. Well-kept grass and budding rose bushes surrounded it. Inside were several rooms with a limited number of beds, medical rooms, very clean doctors' offices, and the office that the social workers used.

I was given a bed in one of the rooms, and the burdens of the ongoing struggle lifted from me. At times, people would stick their heads in the doorway, say "hello", and ask if all was well.

The doctors were polite and extended me a kind welcome. The social workers were some of the most beautiful young girls I had ever seen— smiles, beautiful white teeth, flashing eyes, and long dark hair. I thought for a moment that I might have died, this was heaven, and all were angels. I never had heard of a prison like this.

The rules for living in the clinic were simple. I had to stay in the clinic and not go out the front door. I was on my honor—but I could not wander around the prison.

Outside my room was a small patio where I could find a bit of solitude in a busy crowded place. For some reason, I was kept under an intense security watch. The guards were always checking on my whereabouts. I was even visited in the toilet.

I finally talked to one of the security officers and somehow let him know enough was enough. He then backed his tight observation from my life. Taking this pressure from me helped, but I was taking a beating spiritually as my name entered into the spiritual struggle between the Spanish and English speaking worlds.

Relations with the Department of State in the following months took a decided turn for the worse as various forces pushed and pulled at my stay in prison. I had become a small thorn in the side of good relations between the United States and Mexico.

My visit to the church was a catalyst in a bowl of spiritual unrest. It was growing daily and forcing people to take sides. The Catholic media was seeing to this.

The motives behind the various forces were beyond me, but the action had moved into the mainstream of a deeper river and I was the rock of offense.

The reality of the life of Jesus and how He did nothing but help people, and how at the height of His ministry He was forced to sorrow, humiliation, shame, and death was becoming very real to me. The truth of His words *"Ye shall be hated of all men"* was coming to life. *(Luke 21:17)* Even so, my circumstances were by far much better than those thrust upon Him.

One morning as I passed one of the other rooms in the clinic, there was the judge I had prayed for earlier. His dignity and pride were suffering. He was charged with taking bribes. Over the days and weeks that followed, his pride and dignity gave way to a smile, and a hope that he would soon be out. He agreed that Jesus was his only hope.

At night I would pray. The room would light up with the Spirit of God Almighty, and, like a busy street corner, the spirits and faces of people I knew would well up from the spiritual world which knew no bounds and abide in the pool of heavenly light before me. They would linger and bask in the anointing of Jesus Christ, and then pass on as others took their place. Sometimes this parade would last for hours.

At times Jesus would appear and tell me of things that were going on outside of the prison. My sleep was filled with dreams and spiritual instruction. Jesus would show me things that were to happen the next day. The events would occur, but they would not always take place in a natural way. Jesus would show me what He thought of the situation in a spiritual sense related to His way of thinking.

I was being taken deeper into the spiritual world with the Spirit of Jesus giving me instruction. My contact with the outside world was not as limited in the clinic as it had been in the segregation section. They had a TV, and occasionally I could read a newspaper. I didn't receive any visitors, but was told that a number of Americans had visited the prison to ask of my welfare.

One visitor was my commanding officer from my Air Force days. He was a Mexican-American and had retired to his home in Mexico. I didn't get to see him, but greatly appreciated his interest.

More and more my mind moved and stayed in the spiritual realm. The work to be done in prayer was endless, and here I found a freedom.

The social workers were beautiful and filled with kind love. I think I was starting to fall in love with all of them.

The prison psychiatrist was unusual. I have no doubts that she had the Holy Ghost. She told me she wanted a very good evaluation of me to send to the judge, and he would let me go.

A lot of our sessions centered around the Bible and spirits. She was in a very small percentage of her profession who understood the spiritual world. As we discussed the Bible, she decided I was an extremist. She asked if I saw spirits. I replied that I did. She then told me to draw what I had seen.

I drew some sketches of the spirits Jesus had given me the gift to see. Then she leaned back and questioned me some more in depth. Did I see them often? How did I see them? She then backed away from her desk and said she didn't know what to do.

If she were to show my drawings to the judge, he would say I was crazy and I might never be released. I then reminded her, "Our freedom is in our soul." Jesus had already given me this, and no one could take it away. I never did find out what happened to the reports.

One sunny morning I stopped at the doctor's office. The sincerity of the young doctors was a heartening thing. They were not smiling as I greeted them with a friendly "hello".

The short doctor faced me with a very serious look. They had a problem. The United States Consul Office in Monterrey had been in touch with the prison, and the Consul wanted the Mexican government to hand me over to the United States Government at the border. There, they would, with already given permission and wishes of my family, have a lobotomy performed upon my brain. Here the Mexican doctor became agitated and, with arms waving, said, " The Americans are crazy." He said that I could stay in the prison, and they would not turn me over to the United States. I was stunned. The idea of the lobotomy had come from my own family.

The little doctor's strong words came to me as a voice of the Mexican people. I was reaping as I had sown. Now Mexico was going into the gap of judgment to save me.

In silence I listened, as the doctor told me of the events concerning the effort on the part of the

Department of State in Monterrey to have me turned over to the United States Government at the border.

I had been under constant observation in the clinic for a number of weeks. My spirituality was never in question, as I seemed to be in an area of believers in spirits. They were well aware of the spiritual world. I had not stolen or harmed anyone, and I was not violent. The little doctor said they would protect me. *Thank you, Jesus.*

My father died before I was released from the prison. The Department of State called one day and told me of his death. I loved my dad very much. After talking to the officer from the Department of State, I found a place alone in the large prison yard and wept for an hour or so. Jesus let me know that Dad went to Heaven, and if any work in Mexico helped in any way, then all the hardships were worth it. I think towards the very end of Dad's life he came to an understanding of my strange ways.

I was no longer in the main stream of events, but at the bar of a raging ocean to the north. The gringos had made their move.

I thanked the doctors for taking the stand, which I am sure saved me from a living death. I returned to my room and went to the small patio outside. I could hardly talk. I found a place in the shade, sat down on the cool ceramic tile, and mulled the matter over. It seemed the people of

Mexico would tear into hell itself for what they believed. The ball was in their hands.

~~~~~~~~~~~~~~~~~~

My thoughts went back a number of months to the days preceding my mission to Durango…

The heavy-set Florida state patrolman pulled his cruiser along side of Sherman and asked, "What's going on? What are you doing?"

Sherman was barefooted and had on only a pair of pants. He was running in circles with his hands extending in the air. All this, with a constant muttering of what sounded like a foreign language.

Sherman was exhausted, and a few moments before, Jesus had told him to run in circles and praise His name. (The Lord God Almighty inhabits the praises of His Children. *Psalm 22:3*)

With what was coming, unknown to Sherman, he needed to have a full measure of the indwelling of the Spirit of God.

Sherman was going through a test of radical obedience. He was going to obey what he thought was the voice of God. Nothing else mattered except to obey Jesus and follow Him. *(Genesis 22:1,2)*

The patrolman looked over the roof of his cruiser and guarded himself from what must have seemed to be a deranged wild man.

"You are breaking the law by walking on the

interstate. Why are you here?" the patrolman said. "I am preaching the Gospel and praying for people," Sherman replied.

"Huh," the patrolman echoed. All the while the husky patrolman was adding the situation up. Then he said, "You come with me and I'll take you to someone who needs prayer."

He told Sherman to get in the front seat of the car. As they pulled away, Sherman asked the man if he was saved. The patrolman replied, "I hope so, fellow."

They drove a short distance to the Columbia county jail in Lake City, Florida, with Sherman muttering all the while, and the patrolman glancing sideways at his babbling passenger.

For several days Sherman had been under such a powerful anointing of God that it was impossible for him not to pray in tongues as the Spirit of God gave him utterance. Sherman was praying, and locked in an intense spiritual war.

Now and then he would get a vision of the warfare that swirled around him. The world around him, as he had known it, had passed away, and he was locked in battle with high spiritual powers in another region.

The patrolman pulled up to the front steps of the county jail. Waiting on the steps were the sheriff and several of his men. They were awaiting the patrolman in a spirit of expectation. The patrolman told Sherman to get out, and the patrolman got out on the other side. The sheriff stood wide-eyed, and his neck strained forward as if under some spell.

The patrolman then pointed to the sheriff and spoke to Sherman. "That's the man, pray for him!"

Sherman leveled his right hand, pointed at the sheriff, and began a sharp, crisp roll of God's Language. Tongues were being spoken. The power of God swirled around Sherman like a powerful electric generator.

The spell that had held the sheriff's gaze was gone; he uttered some strong words and jumped back several steps. The highway patrolman nearly doubled with laughter.

The sheriff then ran inside, yelling as he went, "This is the worst case I have ever seen, get the tear gas, get the guns!"

The patrolman was fast after the sheriff as the sheriff fumbled for something to protect himself with. Sherman watched everyone disappear into the central office. He then followed the parade. The highway patrolman caught up with the sheriff and assured him that there was no problem.

Under a wide-eyed stare and a gaping mouth, Sherman passed the sheriff on the way to the large main cell. It was unlocked, and Sherman was motioned inside.

Sherman wasn't the only one motioned inside; that powerful anointing of Jesus Christ was going in with him. Several of the men in the cell jumped

to their feet. Sherman was not much more than a
dumb clown, but whatever was around and
following him was a frightening and terrible thing
to the spirits of these men.

"Sheriff, Sheriff," they screamed, "get this man
out of here!"

One man was so frightened he climbed the bars
on the far side of the large cage. The sheriff stuck
his head around the corner of the bars and paid no
attention to all the yelling and screaming. He
smiled and chuckled; it was good to see the men
hunkered down a bit.

Sherman found a cot. He was glad to have a
place where he could pray and not be bothered.
For several hours he babbled or prayed in tongues.
(1 Corinthians 12)

It was this situation that Sherman's father came
into as a result of a call from the sheriff's office.
"Bob, I want you to go down to the Veterans
Administration Hospital in Gainesville, Florida and
talk to the doctors there," said Sherman's father.

Sherman didn't see any sense in going to the
VA Hospital, but he loved his father and wanted to
honor him and his request. Sherman said, "All
right." Long life is a promise to one who honors
his mom and dad. *(Exodus 20:12)*

It was the visit to the VA Hospital and the
resulting papers that no doubt saved Sherman's life
several times in the prison in Mexico.

Sherman's father paid the $25.00 fine for

walking on the interstate, and Sherman was released into the custody of his father. Away they went to the VA Hospital a few miles to the south.

Sherman was caught away in prayer as they traveled, and he would at times relate some of the visions that he was seeing. His dad was grim and tight-lipped. *What had happened to his son?* He was babbling as if in a trance.

At the VA Hospital, the man in charge of admitting wouldn't heed Dad's request that I be admitted, as there was something very wrong with me. Dad said, "Can't you see, he needs help?"

I sat and babbled.

"He looks all right to me," the man behind the desk said. He looked at me and smiled. Dad turned and wrung his hands in utter frustration at the man behind the desk.

Unknown to my father, the man behind the desk was a member of a Pentecostal type of church and had a gift of tongues. Also, he had an abundance of God-knowledge, and it was clear to him that I was under a very heavy spiritual anointing and not drunk or crazy. I was in pretty good hands. *(Acts 2:15)*

It seemed as if the doors of the VA Hospital were not going to open to me that day, unless Jesus wanted me in this particular place for whatever purpose He had ordained.

All at once I came up out of my chair near the desk and began yelling in tongues and fighting spirits in the air. That was enough. My dad, badly shaken, watched as I was admitted into the hospital.

I was put in the lockup ward and given some pills and shots, which cause you to remain in a state of passive conduct. One couldn't think and just did as one was told. After a few shots and pills I found that I couldn't think. I was tuned out. The pill people had a problem—I was still tuned into the Voice of Jesus. It was at this point that great and amazing things started to happen. Not being able to use my natural mind, I had to rely on the Mind of Christ. *(1 Corinthians 2:16)* I bypassed the natural and asked Jesus what I was to do. Jesus would speak to me and tell me to do this or that, where to go, who to see, and what to say.

After about three or four days of doing what Jesus told me to do, people were saved, healed, and had received the Holy Ghost. One man came to me shaking somewhat violently and asked me to pray for him. His prayer was answered—the shaking stopped. He screamed at the top of his voice, "It works, it works!" and went yelling down the halls, "It works, it works!"

Jesus had come into the nut house with a nut and was moving in a great and wondrous way.

A lady whom I had prayed for when I first arrived at the ward approached me. When I first saw her, her face was greatly twisted and wrinkled. Now, as we talked, she was a different person. Her

face was no longer twisted, and the wrinkles were
gone. "Brother Sherman," she said, "I have
obtained the chapel tonight, and we are having
healing services, and you can come."

What? I thought. *I can come! I'm the one who
brought revival to this place; this is my revival!*
The Lord then spoke to me and said, "No, Bob, this
is <u>My</u> revival."

All right, things have gotten beyond my control.
I went to my room, got down on my knees, and
asked Jesus to get me out of the place.

The man behind the admissions desk had
visited the doctors with his pastor and put in a good
word for me. I was called to one of the doctors'
offices and told that it was best I leave. They had
some people who were very sick, and I had caused
some trouble with my religion. Trying to explain
the Bible to the doctor was like trying to talk to
someone in another world. There was no way.

I decided I had better get out while the getting
was good. I agreed that I should leave.

I was told that I was schizophrenic, but
harmless. The doctors were aware that there were
two definite manifestations of my personality.
They didn't understand it, and my explanations
didn't reach the fellows in the white coats. I tried
to tell them the Spirit of Jesus Christ would
override my natural personality at times. All I
received was a professional, understanding look
and, "Yes, we understand."

They were sure all this had happened to me in the service and I could file for disability. I never did file. I tried to tell them I had been crazy in the service, and now Jesus had let me see what the truth of this world was. I can still hear my dad's words echo, "Yes, Bob, we understand and everything is going to be all right."

~~~~~~~~~~~~~~~~~~

Well, I guess the United States government had all the papers they needed to chop into my head, except they were dealing with some mighty tough people in Durango. Later a member of the United States Consulate in Monterrey visited me, and I was able to see the Veterans Administration medical report, which had followed me from Florida.

The report called speaking in tongues babbling, and praising God a bazaar action. I was harmless, but nuts. The report from the VA rumbled around and through some very high political circles, and each time God's promise to Abraham, *"I will... curse him that curseth thee"* struck home. *(Genesis 12:3)* High powers were being touched on the issue of God's spiritual gifts and the praising of the Almighty God. *(Psalm 105:13-15)* It will take the Day of Judgment for us to know the full truth of what these papers accomplished.

A writer in one of the newspapers in Durango made an observation in his column that "Sherman's van and motorcycle are now with the police", and he wondered what arrangements the chief of police had made with Sherman concerning the confiscation of his van and motorcycle. No doubt, Sherman was beating his head against his cell door thinking up a spell to put on the police. I wrote a letter to the chief giving the van and motorcycle to him. I had no fight with the police. They had been very good to me.

I did warn the chief that there was a curse on the motorcycle. I had not put the curse on the cycle. I felt that a true, powerful, man of God had said a prayer over it, that it only be used for the work of God.

I warned them, whoever rode the motorcycle would fall over dead if it was used for any purpose other than the work of Jesus Christ. One man took the dare to ride the motorcycle. It wasn't long before he was shot in the head as he stopped a man for a traffic violation. I am sure the man had children and a wife.

I was blamed for the policeman's death. I had cursed him. Nothing could have been farther from the truth. I had only tried to warn and help.

After reading the article, I turned my attention to the events of the day. Jesus would have to handle everyone. I now had the faith that the Mexicans were not going to be made fools of or intimidated. We had just passed over the high-water mark of diplomatic efforts by the United States to bury in their minds what was presumed to be an escalating religious war, and to eliminate one of the chief instigators.

At the time I had no way of knowing, but years later I would learn that the push by the Catholic media to vilify me and my actions had caught a moment of spiritual unrest. A backlash of opinions and feelings from many sources had caused idols and statues to be thrown down throughout Mexico. Never did I foresee anything like this happening.

It wasn't my purpose at all. I did not care to become involved in a war or crusade against the Roman Catholic Church. I was being thrust unwillingly and unprepared into a festering wound. Friends and family had forsaken me, and called me crazy. I had not only been written out of my family, but they now stood at the door to, in effect, execute me.

My faith hit the bottom. Maybe I was crazy, maybe this whole thing was a dream. Satan pounded me day and night. I would say, *'What about this,'* or *'What about that, what about all the healings by the Spirit of Jesus I have seen?'* "It doesn't matter," Satan would respond.

It did matter, and the situation I found myself in did matter. Jesus was going to have to do something. Darkness fell over me as I sulked on my small patio. *Where was my God? Where was*

Jesus? I had no visitors, had no letters. The authority of the Catholic media had carried the day. I was a villain.

Overhead, the earthly heavens were filled with large towering thunderclouds. In the distance, I could see the flash of lightning and hear the deep rumble of thunder. Then close by there was a large bolt of lightning, and quickly following a loud clap of thunder that shook the windows. A number of guards gathered at the patio to watch the oncoming storm. An indignant spirit fell upon me concerning the article in the newspaper. If they wanted me to think up a spell, well, I would give them a good one.

I grabbed the mop from the closet in my room and stood on the patio using the mop handle as a rod. I then waved it at the heavens. With the waving of the rod came a mighty bolt of lightning and the following blast of thunder. The high altitude of Durango, with its thin air, enhanced the sound. A war was on.

Again and again I waved my rod at the heavens, and with each wave there was a corresponding flash and loud explosion. I raved somewhat about the police taking my van and all the things that had been said about me. I cackled with a loud maniacal laugh. *"Touch one of God's anointed and see what you'll get!"* I shook that rod! Fear came over the group of guards and they turned and retreated from the madman with the mop handle stirring the heavens.

I pushed the matter to extremes, and after about an hour it was over. Sherman had beaten his head against the heavens. They had their sign.

My faith started growing again. As the storm abated, a vision of Jesus passed overhead. He stretched forth His hand, and a parting bolt of lightning flashed from it and forked before me, hitting the ground. I had heard it was said, it was better to play with forked lightning than to touch one of God's anointed. *(Psalm 105:13-15)*

My hair had been shorn, spiritually speaking, but it was growing back. *One more time Jesus, one more time. (Judges 16:22–28)*

The distractions of the social workers became a problem. They were so beautiful and loving that I was well on the way to falling in love with them all. I wanted to marry all of them, and from the looks and attention I was getting they must have had the same feeling. One morning, one of the beautiful girls appeared and jumped in my bed.

Fear gripping me, I kindly escorted the beautiful young lady to the hallway. All I needed to do to get me killed for sure was to touch one of these beautiful girls.

I had come to Mexico to be a witness for the gospel of Jesus Christ. My conduct had reflected a high degree of character and morals. I would be put to the adobe wall if I became involved with one of the girls. I was at the limit of my temptation. I couldn't take any more.

I asked Jesus for a transfer from the clinic. It wasn't long in coming. Due to a mix up in some orders, I was transferred to the segregation section again.

The sweetness and love of the young social workers was sure close to heaven, but I needed to be about my Father's business.

Before leaving the clinic, Jesus appeared before me with His forehead low, His face set like flint, and His arm uncovered and stretched forth. The chariot of Israel and the horseman thereof....

The cavalry of Israel had arrived astride bolts of lightning with a great noise. The gates of hell had roared forth, they had their day.

The Lord's Day had now come...

Chapter Seven

Back to Segregation

...where sin abounded, grace did much more abound...
Romans 5:20

I gathered my few personal items and blankets, and headed for the segregation section. In some ways, I had become street smart, prison smart, or whatever. There was a way of dealing with the situation I found myself in and making the best of it. No doubt the prison could be a very dangerous place to spend one's life. Perhaps I took ways of survival to extremes, but it was my life. I just didn't take any chances by turning my back on anyone. I cut my own hair—the idea of some fellow snipping around the back of my neck with sharp blades made me feel a bit uneasy. My faith was not strong in these areas. I also learned to walk down the hallway somewhat sideways and keep my back to the wall. On occasions, I would have one or two scuffles before reaching the prison yard. The gringo was always a butt for torment.

Upon my return to the segregation section, I tried to have a Bible study group. This was a joke to the inmates in the now crowded building. They all wanted to fight me. We were not going to talk about anything until I had gone a few rounds with each of them. I didn't think I could take on the whole cellblock one at a time, but I had no other choice. I said, "OK," and we all went outside to the yard. The guards looked on. Jesus was going to have to give me strength. I wasn't a novice at hand-to-hand fighting, but to have to fight the line of men that had now formed in the yard seemed far beyond anything I had ever encountered.

Let's have at it. Big and small they came, one by one. There was no intention of hurting anyone with their fists, just a struggle of strength for their manhood. I did pretty good. Most of the men would come with some form of wrestling learned from watching the antics on the TV wrestling shows.

Years before, I wrestled in amateur sports, and their TV holds were no match for real wrestling holds. I was way ahead in the winning; I sent four or five sailing off into the dust. My strength ebbed, and then a professional armed robber took me down. He pinned me, and the entire group cheered and laughed. I said, "Enough." We would have another go at it the next day.

The next day, sore but rested, I was able to gain the advantage. All right, I was one of them. Everyone shook my hand and patted me on the back. The rites of passage were over.

Willingly and with great sincerity, they would listen to my short messages from the Bible. The meanest and the toughest became as little kids as the Word of God reached their ears and hearts. As

I preached on death and hell, and the lake of fire, and being thrown in alive if you were not with Jesus, the toughest one of the men became very scared. "You mean Jesus is going to throw me in a lake of fire alive? Alive?" he questioned me. *(Revelation 20:15)*

"Alive!" I responded.

He then looked around, and with a deep, strong believing conviction repeated, "Alive," in a soft voice.

Suffering was a way of life with these men, but being thrown into a lake of fire seemed a very harsh thing. When prayer time came at the end of the short sermons, all would remove their hats, get down on their knees, and acknowledge the Great Spirit God of the Universe. On one hand, they were like small children in their simplicity, but some days they could go back to the monsters they had been.

The man who had been touched by the lake of fire and going in alive took a swing at me one day. He hit me on the shoulder. His hand had been loaded with a roll of coins; the coins went spilling down the hallway. Like a kid busting a bag of jellybeans in a crowded school hallway, he got down on his knees, fought and grabbed for his money. Everyone present roared with laughter and teasingly grabbed for his coins. I laughed and teased him more than anyone.

The same man, though he listened and believed

what I said, found it hard to overcome the meanness of his way of life outside the prison walls.

He saved his urine in a large bottle and let it sit for a week, until it had a very vile smell. We had adjoining cells. He had told everyone he was going to toss it on the gringo one night.

'That night' came rolling around. I heard him stir in his cell. Jesus let me know he was going to throw his bottle in my cell at the top of the bars on the wall that separated our cells. I got a small board and waited at the cell bars. Soon, a bottle stuck out of his cell with his hand gripping it tightly. Slowly, his hand moved across the partition between us. I made my move. Wham! I hit the bottle and, crunch! His bottle of stinking urine splashed back on him and broke in his cell.

The lights were off and everyone was locked in their cells, but they had been waiting. Then such cursing as I had never heard broke out from his cell. The entire hallway broke out in laughter. "You had better leave the gringo alone!" they called.

It seemed everyone who came to the segregation section would have a "go" at the gringo. One morning I woke up, and my blanket was on fire. They had tried to get some gasoline and, thank You, Jesus, none was available. The cells were locked with a big padlock in a box outside each cell. In the mornings the guards would unlock our cages and pass on. I was able to obtain a lock, whereby I could lock my door from the inside.

Before this, my shoes and other items would disappear if I overslept. I don't guess you could expect any better considering where all these individuals had come from. Often I could get my possessions back after some begging on my part, or if I promised them a dollar or two. When I got my own lock, I was able to relax in the mornings; the 10x6 suite was all mine.

Winter came with its harshness, but there were no mosquitoes or flies. The bed bugs would scurry about from their homes in the cracks of the walls after the lights went out. They were big, fat and full of blood. The rats and mice ran boldly when darkness fell along the cell row. I obtained some margarine and greased the bars to keep the rats and mice from climbing them and jumping in my bedding. I made a broth of hot peppers and pooled it around my cot. It was all out war.

The first night I watched the rats come up to the pools of hot pepper broth. One sniff and they were off to other places. The stuff made my eyes and nose burn, but it kept the rats away. The men shook their heads in admiration—the gringo was very smart.

I had a cot, but sleeping on it made either my throat or my feet available to be cut through the bars. I moved my bedding to a corner by the toilet, put some old crate slats on the damp cement floor, and slept there. I bought several packages of cigarettes, opened them and sprinkled the tobacco throughout my blankets to keep the bed bugs out. It worked.

My floor was only damp; others had water standing in their cells. It wasn't too bad, but it wasn't a weekend camping trip. Days, weeks, and months were going by. I had reached a point of no return. I couldn't give up and call it quits, and I could only see so far into the future; but even the future looked far off. We were all trapped in time; we had been put on a shelf.

~~~~~~~~~~~~~~~~~

The toilets were flushed from a central knob. At one time, my cell was situated next to this knob, and the water pressure at this point was so strong that it would shoot whatever was in the toilet up in the air and all over the floor. Everyone in the prison had problems. I wasn't alone.

Sometimes these problems were extreme problems. The man who turned the knob that flushed the toilets had his share of problems. He either enjoyed the morning salute of toilets or didn't understand what he was doing. Talking to him about the matter didn't get through. The first time I was awakened by his wet and stinking salvo, I stood helpless and moaned.

After that, I could hear the knob squeaking in

my sleep, and in a second I would grab the piece of cardboard I slept on, along with my blankets, and jump up on the small brick partition that shielded the toilet from the hall. Then the morning salute! After that I would find a broom and clean up. Complaints from inmates about personal abuse were either laughed at or turned aside with a deaf ear. This wasn't a country club. In time, the situation solved itself; the man was transferred.

There was a constant flow of men in the segregation section. Someone who had political influence would be placed here, as opposed to waiting for ten days in a holding room before being put in the general prison, or someone whose safety was in question.

One very cold night, one of the guards told me that 'a brother' was being put in one of the cells near me. He was a Christian policeman, and for some reason had found his way into the prison. I think he had shot someone in the line of duty, but there was a question about the matter, so he was locked up until it was determined how he was to be charged.

He passed by and seemed to know what there was to know about me. It was about lock-down time, and he had no blanket. I had several blankets and felt I needed all of them. He looked at my blankets and asked for one. I said, "Wait a minute." I went to the guard and told him the situation, and he said he would see that the man got a blanket. I should have had better sense about getting a blanket during the rush hour crunch of lock down.

Many times the guards, in the rush of daily cares, would forget such requests, and I should have thought of this. Just before the lock-down came, and no blankets had arrived, I did hand the policeman a thin blanket. It was cold, and 'the brother' weathered the chilly first night. He gave my thin blanket back to me the next day as he left. A year passed before I saw him again. He had gotten a job in the coffee house as a cook. It was a very cold morning, and the area behind the counter was very warm. Outside in the room it was cold.

I asked him if I could come behind the counter and get warm. No one was in the place, and I thought it would be all right. He became upset and said that I must not come behind the counter. I stayed on the other side, away from the big wood burning stove, and chilled it out. It was then that I learned a great lesson. I felt about as big as a bug. I had not made it comfortable for this man, but I had not let him freeze either.

I thought I had done him a favor by giving him the thin blanket. Now *I* was getting the thin blanket treatment. I was reaping sparingly. I thought to myself, *If I had given and made something of a sacrifice with my other blankets, I am sure I would have been asked to come near the wood stove. (2 Corinthians 9:6)* 'The brother' took none of my thoughts in; the only thing he was concerned about was keeping his job. I was reaping as I had sown—sparingly.

There were several other times when I was asked to give a buck or two and I didn't. The rejected request stuck sideways in my throat. I still get a tinge of remorse when I think about it, even to this day.

~~~~~~~~~~~~~~~~~~

Some men were driven to near insanity by the harshness of the segregation section. One young man, Toluco, would sit and slice himself with a razor. One morning, I counted twenty-five or thirty slices on his arms and chest. Each had a stitch or two and oozed blood and body fluids. Tuluco was a demoniac.

Toluco had a heart that was pure gold. His profession was that of a pickpocket. He would boast that he was the greatest pickpocket in all of Mexico. I had to remind him that he had to be the second best, as the best had not been caught.

From time to time, I would get lessons on how to pick pockets and succeed in life. At other times, different men would add things about their profession. They would demonstrate the best way to kill a person, or brag about the money that had been turned their way in crime. For the gringos in the prison, it was like a business convention. They met men who represented the various drug dealers from all over Mexico. The overriding fact, though, was that all had ended their professional careers in disaster behind bars.

The drug smuggling business was very simple. You either bought off or killed off anyone in your way, police or otherwise. After listening to some of the tales of crime and slaughter, I would stagger back to my cell shaking my head. The odors of hell's kitchen hovered heavily overhead.

Toluco received the Holy Ghost. He would go up and down the halls singing in tongues. He loved Jesus. His cutting of himself stopped as Jesus began to move in his life. He printed *Jesus is coming soon* on his T-shirt. Toluco had other problems, though. He was a glue sniffer. He would have a little bottle of glue with a straw stuck through the top. He would sip his way into a slow brain burn. One day, he was staggering around the prison yard out of his mind, drunk on glue vapors. I chided him. He then cried, said he wasn't good enough for Jesus, and cut the words *Jesus is coming soon* out of his T-shirt.

All he had on now was a rag with a big hole. He didn't want to hurt Jesus. I wished I had shut my big mouth.

Some of the men declared war on the rats one morning. They flooded the holes in the floor and beat the wet, poor things with yells and screams and great excitement as they were forced out of their homes. Toluco kept his cell locked and would

not permit anyone to kill the rats that ran for safety
in his cell. "The rats are my friends," he said.
Toward the end of my stay in Mexico, he was
released. I didn't see him again, but he had come
to know Jesus.

~~~~~~~~~~~~~~~~~

During my entire stay in the prison with all the
harsh physical circumstances, when I remained
focused on the work for Jesus, the hardships had a
minimal effect on my life. I was free in my soul,
and the joy of the Lord was my strength.
(Nehemiah 8:10) If I lacked joy, I asked Jesus to
fill me with joy. He would answer. "Happiness
from external sources isn't a needed factor; the
inward joy given by the Spirit of Jesus Christ is the
needed strength."

There were times when my courage and boldness
failed me; at these times I would ask to be filled
with courage. Courage would come. Some faith I
had obtained came as a gift. *(1 Corinthians 12:9)*
In these instances I found that I could pray for a
fever, and the fever would leave. This particular
faith just came. I had no faith, and then I did after
seeing the immediate results of praying, or what
would come by revealed faith.

Another gain I made by faith was growing faith.
(Galatians 5:22) On many points of faith, I started
growing. I was well aware of the presumptuous

faith, faith that you presumed was in the will of God, maybe or maybe not. I tried my best to search in prayer for the will of God, and then, once finding His will, I would throw all my faith into prayer.

There was a chill in the morning air as I made my way to the small yard outside the segregation section. I found a sunny place to lean against the wall. The sun was our only source of heat. I had been there a few minutes when a man burst out of the door leading to the yard. His eyes were bulging, and he was breathing hard. He glanced around the yard, stopping when his eyes came to rest on me. Whatever his problem was, it became evident that he considered I was either part of it, or the cause. Events moved so fast that I could only watch in silence. He let out a couple of loud whoops and came at me. In the process, he picked up the largest rock he could find in the rock strewn, dusty yard. It was about the size of a small basketball. Other men in the yard gathered quickly with him. He rushed at me with the boulder held high over his head. The gathering men formed a semi-circle around me, with this fellow with the big rock high over his head just a few feet away.

It was Mexico against the United States in the minds of those gathered with him. Judgment for the good old U.S.A. now became the order of the hour.

I couldn't say, "Help me Jesus" or anything, but I was at peace with my emotions. I did think the situation was bad, but more than anything, I wondered just how I was going to get out of this one. I didn't know, but with an inner assurance, I felt I would.

With a boulder aimed squarely at my head and this crazed man in front of me, surrounded by other crazies, I thought to myself, "How is Jesus going to get me out of this one?" I had faith He would, somehow.

Then a very unusual thing took place. Two spiritual powers appeared behind and on each side of the group. I had a small stick in my hand about a foot long. My arm went up without me lifting it, foot-long stick and all. Then there was a blast of white, spiritual smoke, and fire extended from the small stick. The men were stunned, and the big guy dropped the boulder at his feet and stood, arms dangling at his side, stunned.

The entire incident scared me, but not enough to keep me from rapidly walking through the dazed bunch to a place away from any more encounters. *(Luke 4:30)* Jesus had ministering angels there all the time. I am sure these angels had worked, unknown to me, to save me before. This time, He let me see them. The Greatness of God, The Greatness of God! This was all I could think. Praise for the Almighty came from down deep in my soul.

At another time, in another section of the prison, I walked into a room. A man saw me come in, jumped up and sneered, "Sherman!" Before another word was spoken, he lunged at me. He took a step or two and then collapsed on the floor. He died the next day. I was able to minister to the man that night as he struggled for his life. I did feel he received me before he died. Deathbed salvation? Yes! Another thief on a cross.

I had seen angels around me before, at times, and the large swords they carried were very impressive, to say the least. No doubt this man purposed to harm me, and I could only believe he was hit in the head with one of those shining swords held by the angels who stood guard around the clock to ensure my safety.

It was Christmas Eve, and it passed as any other day. There were no religious frills in the segregation section. Many of the people present were partly out of their minds from natural causes, and I do think the others stayed high on one thing or the other. I stayed to myself, praying most of the time, and reading the Bible. Everyone knew by now; they only came out on the bad end by tormenting the gringo. Many called me a witch doctor. Whatever, I enjoyed the peace and respect it brought. It was just better to leave the gringo alone.

Christmas morning arrived. It was very cold,

and I wrapped up in my blankets and shivered. Then a group of men appeared at my cell door. They were shouting and banging on my cell bars.

"Jesus, Jesus," they shouted and pointed to the outside doorway. The din became louder, and several other men appeared and joined the shouting. I had to get up. It was clear they were not going away unless I got up. I thought with all the shouting and noise, perhaps they had seen Jesus walking outside.

I followed the shouting group outside. "Jesus, Jesus," they yelled, and pointed. Over the entire grounds of the prison was one of the most beautiful sights I had ever seen. So simple, but so beautiful; a two inch blanket of white, pristine, powder covered everything.

In a materialistic society, the snow would have gone unnoticed, but to everyone at the prison, it was a clear sign from God. Jesus was King, and He had passed overhead. A spirit of humility came over all in the prison, and many hearts were turned to the King that day. Signs and wonders were following. *(Mark 16:20)*

~~~~~~~~~~~~~~~~~~

The man with whom I had so much trouble, the one who got so upset about the lake of fire, tamed down a good bit. One day as I watched a young kid torment him, I heard him say with an intimidating voice, "You had better leave me alone, I am a man of God."

My way of reaching these men was not the standard church way, but they were being reached and snatched from hell. These were extreme conditions, and it took extreme measures to deal with such.

The days, weeks, and months moved by with a steady pace. I watched the entire proceedings and God's Work with awe and wonder. The streets of Durango and the Catholics seemed in another world.

Jesus gave me a warning that the shadow of death had come over the segregation section. Often at night Jesus would appear at my cell door. This greatly strengthened my faith. I received two warnings. A great man of God came as a spirit through the bars, talked to me, and warned me that two men had planned to kill me. *(Acts 10:22)* The other warning came as a sign. I heard in the Spirit a rattling from the showers at the end of the hall. The rattling was that of a rattlesnake about to strike. A few days later a man called Paco would confirm the warning.

How would I get out of this place I didn't know, but I would. First things first. I needed to get locked up where no one could get close to me. Very calmly, under the leading of Jesus Christ, I walked downstairs to the main room, found a broom, and swept all the trash in the main room into the guard's office. Then I waited. The large guard in charge rounded the hallway corner and stood in an examining silence. I stood with a broom in hand and smiled at him. He exploded. "Fifteen days in solitary for you, you so and so gringo!" he yelled.

With that he grabbed me, and away we went to a nice cell with locks on it. Spirits of claustrophobia attacked me in a way I had never experienced. I saw how very easy it would be to go off the deep end if you didn't know Jesus. I backed against a wall repeating, "Jesus, Jesus, Jesus." A darkness in the cell cleared out. Deep in the inner prison of the inner prison, Jesus was still with me; all was well with my soul.

In a few days, a team of guards inspecting the section came by. They decided that I shouldn't be in such a condition and ordered me transferred to the main prison. Jesus had made a way of escape. He indeed was the Way Maker.

A few weeks later, the shadow of death moved into the segregation building and waited. As if by a signal, the snake struck, and death wrapped itself around its victim.

Chapter Eight

The Trials

*But when they deliver you up, take no thought how or what
ye shall speak: for it shall be given you in that same hour
what ye shall speak. Matthew 10:19*

It is not my purpose, by expounding on the
various times that I was brought before the judicial
officials of Mexico, to crusade against the legal
system of Mexico.

On most occasions, I was treated with respect
and courtesy. The Mexican officials did the best
they could, considering all factors.

It became very evident that the Lord Jesus
wanted me in the prison for an ordained period of
time, and woe unto the forces which would seek to
change His purpose.

There was a process I had to endure through to
reach the point where I was committed to the
prison for whatever term that Jesus cared to be
ordered.

I resigned myself to take whatever came with
lightness, knowing that Jesus knew the time and
date I would come out of prison.

The first time I was brought before the judicial
official, it was for a hearing on the matter of guilt
or innocence. My name was called over the
loudspeakers around the prison, and I was told to

report to the main office. At each gate, I would repeat the orders I had received, and would be allowed to pass through the several gates that sealed off the various sections of the prison.

I smelled. My T-shirt, pants, and jacket were well worn and dirty. I was bearded and wild-eyed. A dirty, flat-topped cowboy hat that I picked up somewhere wobbled on top of my head. I must have been a sight. Bitterness and anger about the entire situation festered within me. I wasn't the nicest fellow to be around.

The vintage blue, police paddy wagon from town rolled to the main door of the prison, and all of the condemned were jammed into the rear of the van. Away we went to the city of Durango and the Office of Justice. It was a very trusting situation—no chains or handcuffs. The rear door opened, and I was once more in the streets of Durango. We followed the policeman up a flight of stairs and found space along the walls of the waiting room to sit down. One or two policemen patrolled the hall and waiting room. As long as you stayed still, no one was upset and the security was very loose.

One day, one of the Americans bolted from the rear door of the paddy wagon when it was opened down town. He made his escape from the area, but was picked up later that day at a restaurant. He was about six-feet-five and clearly stood out in a crowd. The men who caught him pulled him into the street and beat him with their gun butts. It wasn't a merciful beating. He couldn't move for days.

One man, who had escaped from the prison before and was recaptured, escaped from the judge's office a second time. He answered the call to load the paddy wagon for the trip to the judicial office in rags, a large old hat, sandals, and very dirty. Meekly he found his place in the judicial waiting room. Then, in a very humble way, he asked one of the policemen if he could use the toilet.

He went to the toilet, stripped off his outer clothes quickly, put on hidden clean clothes and shoes, washed his face, combed his hair, and with a handful of legal papers, walked briskly past the guarding policeman outside. The freedom was short-lived; the man was picked up one night as he visited his family. The guards from the prison had put a "stakeout watch" at his house.

My name was called, and I was ushered into a room containing a desk with several chairs before it. On the desk was the message of warning I had nailed to the door of the cathedral, and the hammer I had used and left outside.

I was told that the man behind the desk was the judge's secretary, and he would take notes of what I had to say and give them to the judge with his evaluation. I was told the man behind me was my lawyer. I wasn't the easiest man to deal with.

"Yes," I said, I was guilty of the charges of

preaching on the street and shoving over the government property, but I didn't hit the government property (the statue) with the hammer. Someone else had beaten the head off the small statue after the confrontation in the cathedral.

The secretary took a few notes, then told me he would study the information and make his report to the judge. I was informed that the judge wanted to see me. He had told one of the Americans in the prison he wanted to help me.

I was escorted to the judge's office. Behind a very large desk sat the judge, a tall man with a balding head. I was told to sit down. The judge could speak English. The Holy Ghost manifested at this time, and I could see a very large devil above the judge, hanging on tight. Then my arm flew up, thrusting my Bible in the judge's face. I said, "You had better listen to what I have to say or God is going to destroy Durango." The words were not mine; Jesus had come in and taken control of the situation and me.

The judge was taken aback by the audacious gringo. He sputtered, and then said, "I can see we are not of the same spirit." With a wave of his hand, I was led from the room.

Later, this judge was transferred to a city in Mexico, which was greatly damaged by earthquakes. Durango was spared. I often wondered if he remembered the crazy gringo waving the Bible in his face.

Under the Mexican legal system, I would either be charged guilty or innocent. If I were declared to be guilty, then I would be bound over for a trial. It did not take much study of the situation to understand why gringos were not granted bonds of release.

The main charge against me was the spirit of violence that I had expressed by the supposed hammering the head off the statue in the cathedral. The authorities were rightly concerned about public violence, but there was ample evidence that the doll had a sound head after I was escorted from the church. A newspaper in Mexico City ran a story concerning the incident, publishing in the article a picture of the small statue undamaged except for the hands, which were damaged in its fall.

The local newspapers, which were published later, ran a headline front-page story with a picture of the head smashed, and the hammer I had left outside. The Catholics were up in arms against the supposed display of violence.

It didn't matter, as Jesus was going to have His way. TV, radio, and newspapers had thrust the small incident into the political and public arena, forcing people to take firm stands for or against my conduct and me.

Rome was on a roll and I wasn't far from being flattened. The Mexican Government was going to 'hang tough' with the situation. I had to admire the fortitude or just plain guts that the nation of

Mexico displayed against the giant to the north.

I was declared guilty and was ordered to stay in the prison until my trial.

I didn't know of the efforts to secure my release which were going on outside the prison, but I was aware that the struggle had moved to another level, and I was caught between the efforts of the United States State Department to protect their citizens and Mexico's 'Hang Tough Law' with the gringos.

I had been informed of the State Department's efforts to deliver me to the United States authorities to have a hole bored in my head, so I joined sides with the Mexican 'Hang Tough Law.' As far as I was concerned, they could hang as tough as they wanted to.

I wasn't in any hurry to get to the border. I came to Mexico to tell people about Jesus and His Way. What a wonderful opportunity was before me! Perhaps not everyone looked at it in this manner.

The church organization that had helped me greatly was under pressure by the government of the United States concerning my actions. The Vietnam War was going strong. People who had come to the United States from Cuba were launching raids against Castro, and training small armies in Florida to harass the Castro government in Cuba. Laws had been passed with harsh penalties for aiding the overthrow of another government from the shores of the United States, and the requirements of the 501(c)3 tax exempt IRS Law pressed heavy with its intimidation. Bow or burn.

The event of the doll falling to the floor was being stretched to the limits and beyond. I had attacked the church with a hammer, and all churches in Mexico were government property. It was believed I was in revolt against the government of Mexico, and was being funded from the United States by the charity of the organization of which I was a member. How my life ever got to this point I didn't know, but it seemed insanity was having its day.

I thought of Jesus and all He endured before the determinate council the night before He went to the cross *(Matthew 26:57 & 27:1),* the insanity of His situation, and then the horrible lashings and beatings He passed through on the way to the cross. *(Matthew 27:26-31)* I knew I was only scratching the surface of ungodly afflicted suffering, yet my physical and mental strength was being strained to the breaking point.

A young friend from the church of which I was a member visited me, and here I weathered the unkindest cut of all. 'Et tu, Brute!' And you also... I had endangered the church organization by my actions. I was told to co-operate with the Judicial Officials, and in a short time, I would be set free. He then spent a day visiting the officials in

Durango, and apologizing for my conduct. The
whole matter was 'unfortunate'. Rome knew no
boundaries. I was denied thrice.

The young man visited me again the next day.
I told him that I resigned from the church
organization, and that put an end to anything he
had to say concerning my actions. I thanked him
for his efforts on my behalf, and assured him that
the organization he was associated with thought
they were doing the proper thing by sending him. I
encouraged him to return and work hard for Jesus.
*"You shall be hated of all men for my name's
sake"* was hitting home. *(Matthew 10:22)* That
sharp sword of division had cut to the quick.
(Luke 12:51)

My family felt I was insane. The church
organization I had been affiliated with had serious
questions about my sanity, and the Catholic Church
considered me a villain and a threat to God's work.
Two nations considered me to be an insane
criminal. I took my Bible, got down on my knees,
put both arms around God's Holy Word, and told
Jesus that He was all I needed and I would stand on
His Word.

Was I to be ground into the dust? It sure
appeared this way. It seemed the only person I
now had left as a friend was Jesus, but He was all I
needed. I didn't leap for joy, but I sure had a
wonderful feeling inside.

Strange things were going on inside the city of

Durango. Rome had pushed me into a light of martyrdom. Their efforts to vilify me were starting to backfire. The people of Durango, particularly the young people, weren't buying the media circus.

Upon leaving the judge's office on one visit to sign papers, a group of the office workers appeared and asked me to sign various pieces of paper. They wanted my autograph; here were those beautiful Mexican girls again. Angels were everywhere. I asked the two policemen who escorted me if I could return and talk with the Angels. How kind they were. They smiled and said; "Sure."

I always carried a pocketful of prayer cloths with 'Jesus' printed on them in large letters. As Paul had faith in his aprons and handkerchiefs, I had faith in the small pieces of coarse cloth with the Name of our Great God, Jesus, written in large, bold, red letters. *(Acts 19:12)* I passed out the cloths to the small group. They said they wanted my name, but I assured them the name of Jesus was of much more value. With such sweetness they agreed.

Down the stairs, and out to the truck—I passed a young man I knew, and he shook my hand and encouraged me. One of the policemen remarked that Sherman sure did have a lot of friends.

When we got back to the prison, my spirit was greatly lifted. I bought the two policemen a soda, thanked them, shook their hands, and departed into my inner world with smiles all around.

My acceptance by the young people at the judge's office was only the tip of a growing spiritual iceberg. The people of Durango had not been fooled or pressured by the Roman Nation, which had come to dominate and control their lives from cradle to grave.

Theirs was a constant spiritual cry; "Jesus yes, Rome no!"

The day of my trial rolled around. I was called to report to the paddy wagon for the ride down town and my long awaited trial. We arrived at the judge's office, and I was stacked with some others around the waiting room. A young policeman with a rifle sat next to me.

My name was called in a roll check, and I raised my hand. The name 'Sherman' brought him to life. He looked at me and quickly slammed a bullet into the chamber of his rifle. "You make one false move and I will put you away," he said. He didn't want my autograph. I didn't even move my head sideways as long as he was there.

The door to the trial chambers opened, and a young man stuck his head out and read from a list, "Sherman." The trial was on and over in about ten minutes. I had my say. Then, my old friend, the *padre* from the cathedral, sat next to me and had his say. He had changed a lot. He wasn't the raging judo expert I had encountered in the cathedral. Now, I could see the pupils in his eyes, before they had been black orbs. He told his story.

Then an assortment of men who had been present that day sat and told their story. Their stories conflicted. One said I had a hammer. The hammer was still the bone of contention. I pointed to a photograph in one of the newspaper articles placed in evidence, which showed the head of the small statue intact. It didn't matter, as I was clearly guilty.

Then the testimonies were completed, and I was told that I would be notified of the resulting decision by the judge. Many thought I had suffered enough, and should be let go and sent to the United States. Others thought I should be hanged.

After a week or so, I was notified that I had been found guilty and sentenced to six years in prison. Jesus had been nailed to the cross. Rome had carried that day only to seal its doom in eternity.

The charges and decision went on to a higher court. Then an unusual thing happened; the next judge reversed the decision, and the case was sent back to Durango. The higher judge ruled that since no value had ever been placed on the statue, it didn't have a value, so there was no loss to the state.

The matter was finally decided against me after a few members of even higher courts made their voices known. Right or wrong, I was staying in Mexico. The evidence didn't matter; I was guilty. I had, long before this, begun to pay very little attention to all the legal maneuvering and results. Jesus was in control, and no earthly power was going to change His course. It was still one day at a time, sweet Jesus.

Shortly after the judgment of my stay in the prison had been pronounced, one of the officials of the prison came to the dorm where I lived and made a speech, highlighting the fact that "Your freedom is in your soul."

This was a surprise to me; I was reaching authorities in a way I had not expected. In a light manner of conversation, the Truth was moving and not returning void. I had closed a gap between my brothers in bondage. I was more a brother of suffering than a gringo.

Chapter Nine

The Streets of Mexico

For I am with thee, and no man shall set on thee to hurt thee: for I have much people in this city. Acts 18:10

I sat in reflective silence. The high blue Mexican sky looked down on the gringo hunkered on his dry stubble. Remembrances, remembrances. Days had moved by with the daily birth of events.

You had to be somewhere, and if the prison was to be my lot, then OK. The main thing was that I stay in the will of God. This might be a hard thing for some to understand. I had reached a point where their understanding it or not didn't matter. What mattered was the good warm feeling in my soul.

Events had passed me to this point. The ministry in the streets, the jail downtown, the hundreds of people I had met in the name of Jesus, the Catholic Church, the clinic, Paco's confrontation, and Segregation. Durango was over the high wall to the west several miles. This seemed to be a good time to call the dance to a halt. Not so, and an even greater struggle must lie ahead.

For a man of God, there is always a greater struggle ahead. In the spiritual world, the various levels of evil who rule this world fly at the light of Jesus Christ in one with the Baptism of the Holy

Ghost. They come to test and try the man of God. Is he really a man of God? Jesus felt the full force of testing when the light of God came forth in Him. Doubt is one of the big tests Satan will throw. Doubting the Word of God—the original sin.

I had come through the Segregation gate and up the long cement sidewalk, the gray mile. I felt like a free man somewhat. In the main prison I was in Mexico, and each day brought with it a fresh insight into the people who made up this diverse nation.

At this point in time, it would have been difficult for any person or authority to get me to leave. From morning to night, characters and events swirled around me with such interest and attraction, that even Hollywood could study in awe and interest and not find a screen wide enough to contain the show, nor the finances to put it on.

The authorities asked me where I would like to live. By accident or God's purpose, I selected the wrong cell to live in.

One of the officers and the man I picked out to live with had a hard-core vendetta going. I didn't know this at the time. Someone had entered the young officer's home and brutally killed two of his younger brothers. The murder embittered him and swayed his feelings towards the men in the prison. He was always on the lookout for that man.

Me living with the opposite side brought a gap between this officer and myself, which hadn't been there. I don't believe the gap was ever closed as long as I stayed in the prison.

I had nothing but admiration for the conduct of the men who ran the prison. I pushed them. I pushed them hard. Stubbornness? I'm not sure, but I wasn't a happy camper.

They had about one thousand men, the large part of them potentially violent, on their hands. If the TV broke down, it became an all out emergency to get the thing fixed as soon as possible. They didn't want the uneasy peace upset by anyone or anything. When the guards used their authority to discipline someone, it was done swiftly with all authority. If there was a sadistic spirit among the officers and guards, it manifested itself rarely.

There did come a time when a small group of guards joined to break me of my faith in The Lord Jesus Christ and His Word. I felt there was an outside pressure that motivated them.

I was placed in a cell in the bowels of the dorm which was to be my home, jammed next to the large dining room and along the single entrance to this area. Everyone came and went by my cell. I felt like the main attraction in a zoo.

Days, weeks, and months were flying by. The prison never ceased to be a wonder of characters— jewel thieves, bandits, gang leaders, murderers, street thieves, armed robbers, drug traffickers, smugglers, white-collar criminals, rustlers, policemen, pickpockets, and even a whole tribe of Indians complete with white pajama dress and wide brimmed, flat-top hats. The government helicopter had landed in their fields as they cultivated drug plants, rounded them up, and away they went in the helicopters from high in the mountains to the prison in Durango. They were a sight.

Each man had a story to tell. It had to be a good one, as his life was as important to him as mine was to me.

The men in the prison were from all over Mexico. "Where are you from, where are you from?" I always asked.

"I am from Michocan."

"I am from Veracruz." Or, "I am from Durango."

They would always swell with pride as they spoke of their home state or city.

When it came to asking what their sin was, it was a different story. I couldn't understand why everyone said he was a murderer. After a while, it dawned on me that the killers in the prison were at the top of the banana stalk in respect. So, many secured themselves regardless of their crime by saying he was a murderer. Not many people bothered them. On the other hand, others claimed they had been framed or were innocent. As a person became more committed to the idea of not getting out, he would drop all pretenses.

One man jerked his shirt open and stood bare-

chested before me. "See these bullet wounds?"
Five or six ugly scars were sunk across his chest.
"That guy emptied his pistol on me. Then I pulled
my gun and shot him through the head." He then
said, "Jesus kept me alive."

While taking a shower one day, a well-scarred
individual glanced sideways at me. With a small
sneer of contempt he stated, "Gringo, you don't
have any bullet holes or knife scars; how come?" I
thought for a minute. Then I pointed to an old knee
operation scar and my hernia operation scar and
said, "Don't worry, fellow, I got 'em." He grunted
a silent approval.

I asked Santos, the leader of a bandit gang, how
he got caught. He said, "We stopped this small
Volkswagen one night north of Durango. The
driver was the Catholic bishop of a large city in
Mexico." He then told how one of his men walked
over to the car, stuck a pistol in the window, and
shot the fellow in the head for no reason.
"Someone got our tag number as we left, and the
soldiers tracked us down. Man, did we ever get
worked over!" I later asked Mirana—the fellow
who did the shooting—why he shot the bishop. He
shook his head bewilderedly and, slowly pondering
the subject, said, "I don't know."

According to God's Law today, if you, in your
heart, kill a person, steal, lust, or violate the rule of
'Do unto others as you would have them do unto
you', you sin as surely as if you do it. *(Matthew 5:28)*

I wasn't an innocent person among these guilty and condemned men. Jesus traced my sins in the dust that day as the harlot faced the stoning pit. *(John 8:1-11)*

Once a month, a judge from town would come to the prison. All would gather. The list of the men in the prison would be called. I would raise my hand and say "Present" when my name was called. Everyone held the list in high regard. If you wanted to say something, you could speak to a judge directly. I often thought of that final roll call of God Almighty and His Great White Throne. *(Revelation 20:11-15, 2 Corinthians 5:10)*

Regardless of my feeling about being innocent, I was a guilty human being and could ask for nothing except mercy, mercy. "Lord, have mercy upon me. I'll do better and I'll do the making up." For sure, my hands and arms were covered with the blood of innocents and all my garments stained. *(Jeremiah 2:34-37)* I needed to do redemption work.

The food in the prison was good. From time to time we would get a pork chop, some meat, or fish. Most always a slaughtered cow was brought in for the noon meal. The cooks would chop it up and put it in a stew. The stew made the day. Tortillas, the ever-present beans, steaming brown rice, and a cinnamon or rice drink with the stew made for a meal. If you had a buck or two, you could buy an egg or a can of tuna fish from the small grocery store.

I would buy a large jalapeno pepper for the noon or supper meal. Then it was a tight walk back to the dining room; I'd hold the pepper in one hand, cock my fist with the other, and walk fast. Along the way, nearly always, someone would try to take it from me, or knock it out of my hands. I'd fight and kick my way to the dinner table. What a place to live in!

Even with all the craziness of the place, I must say I enjoyed it. The joy of the Lord was my strength. *(Nehemiah 8:10)*

The authorities told me I could preach in the prison. I didn't do too good trying to reach the people by preaching on the prison streets. I was given permission to work my trade, though. I thought this sure was a crazy, mixed up place. "Yes, you can preach in here, we have freedom here," I was told. *Freedom,* I thought. *Preaching is the reason I'm in here—oh well, it's a crazy world.*

The prison, in my mind, became my parish. Regardless of all the wonders and the excellent performance of the guards, we were still playing hardball.

One scripture that Jesus had given me to hold on to was the 140th Psalm, verses eight and nine. *"Grant not, O Lord, the desires of the wicked: further not his wicked device; lest they exalt themselves. Selah. As for the head of those that compass me about, let the mischief of their own lips cover them."*

There were times when spirits would come so hard against my forehead that I nearly could physically jerk them off. On several occasions, my faith was all but blotted out of my mind. The only scripture I could remember was, *"Surely goodness and mercy shall follow me all the days of my life." Psalm 23:6* This was enough. I would then go around singing this short verse all day.

Then, like one climbing a ladder, I would add another scripture to my memory, then another, and slowly, rung by rung, I would pull my mind back to Jesus by His written Word and Spirit.

The intense efforts by various powers to either get me to the States or incite action against me in the prison were on the wane. The war in Vietnam was over. Nixon's problems were over. There was a new President in the United States, and a new President coming to office in Mexico.

On one occasion, a young American missionary visited me. He was a true man of God, but I felt his spirit of condemnation towards my actions and me was not just. They did reflect the feelings of the community of American missionaries in Mexico about my situation.

"Yea, you nearly got us all kicked out of Mexico." Just where people's minds were I didn't know, but he was in violation of the laws of Mexico preaching as he was doing. He condemned my beard and the poor rags I used for clothes. I told him we didn't have hot water to shave with, nor did I have the money to buy shaving stuff, and I had no apologies for my clothes or the message painted on my jacket. *Get real, man,* I thought. *You're doing the same thing that I received a jail sentence for doing, and you sit there running my harsh circumstances and me in the mud.* I don't think I ever got over the bashing from the organized church world.

I felt more at home with the bandits than the church people. Bitter? No, but Jesus was opening my eyes to the reality of life.

~~~~~~~~~~~~~~~~~

People were going and coming all the time in the dormitory where I lived. One day a young fellow arrived from the United States. Somehow he had been tracked down and caught in Chicago. I think his sin was "murder one". Most of the men who were in the prison for killing someone were pretty trustworthy people as long as they were not pushed too much, and if forces came along to push them, well, they got a strange look on their face, their eyes narrowed, and it was best to move on to somewhere else if at all possible when this strange look came around.

I often wondered what would happen if someone threw in a couple of boxes of pistols fully loaded. The devil would have had a run on the place.

One morning I passed the cell of the new fellow from Chicago. He had that strange look on his face, and Jesus spoke to me and told me that Satan had purposed to kill me through this man. He lived three cells from me. This didn't help my situation any, and I decided he was going to get healed of this problem if we were going to have to live together under such confining circumstances. He was going to get healed even if he didn't want or ask to be healed.

Two months or thereabouts later, a number of the men had gathered and were talking about the supernatural and spirits. The man from Chicago was present. One man asked me if I saw spirits. "Yes," I replied. I then told the man from Chicago that Jesus had told me about a spirit which had tried to get him to kill me about two months back. He looked at me with mild amazement and said, "Yes, I was going to kill you then, but it all passed my mind; how did you know?"

I said, "Jesus told me."

Thank God for Jesus and His overcoming power. As a result of the revelation of the man's heart, he turned to Jesus. *(1 Corinthians 14:24,25)*

~~~~~~~~~~~~~~~~~

The Americans in the prison were all in on drug charges. Most were young men who had been picked up with small amounts of various drugs. Every now and then a 'biggie' would come in. These fellows were hard, slick, and they knew the ropes. The only thing about their ropes was that the end of the rope was behind prison bars.

Towards the end of my stay in Durango, a 'biggie' from California was put in the prison. Anyone in the drug trade had blood on their hands, whether they knew it or not. This man from California was said to have had contracts put out on several Mexican narcotics agents. The agents had been murdered.

One group of drug dealers had a large aircraft. Once a month they would go through an area and pick up anyone whom they perceived as a threat, or someone they disliked. They would shoot them, load up their large aircraft with the bodies, fly out over the Pacific Ocean for several hundred miles, and unload. It was a very silent war between the Drug Enforcement Agency and the drug dealers. Sometimes it wasn't so silent.

The new fellow from California was big-time, and I could never bring myself to trust anything he had to say. One of his big complaints was that the Mexican prison was not at all like an American prison. "Why, at Long Beach we had clean sheets every day." He spoke of the prison at Long Beach, California.

It seemed he lived more on the edge of destruction than I did. I don't know if he ever changed his way. He lived in another area, and I was glad he did.

Two young Americans were flying back to the United States from Mazatlan when their small aircraft ran low on fuel as they passed over Durango. They landed at an airfield near Durango, refueled, and almost made a safe exit. Not so, as Jesus had His Hand on the flight.

As they gunned the engines for the takeoff on the small strip, the Federal Police ran alongside them with large machine guns aimed at the cockpit. The engines went to idle, the five hundred pounds of marijuana they had on board was unloaded, and both came into the prison.

One of these young men was from the small town in Florida where I had taught school some years before. Some people I had known had invited him to a prayer meeting. It was the same prayer meeting I had attended when I lived in Florida.

Someone said a prayer, and later the fellow ended up behind bars in my 'church'. Then some people from this prayer group came down to visit us. The visit didn't hurt, and it helped in a deep spiritual way. When I left, I could see no outward sign of any breaking of a hardness of spirit in this fellow, but something must have been touched down deep. Small world. I am sure Jesus knows what He is doing. God's Word will not come back void, and the young man had heard God's word. *(Isaiah 55:11)*

The large group of Indians who were put in the prison for growing marijuana in their fields were different from the criminals somewhat. They didn't want to harm anyone; all they wanted was to be able to grow whatever they could sell in their fields so they could eat.

On some of them, I could see the spiritual promise of God, which was their heritage from the work of the Franciscans several centuries before. *"For the promise is unto you, and to your children..." (Acts 2:39)* The Franciscans had done a work for Jesus unhindered by Rome.

Cortez asked the king of Spain for a group of Franciscans to be sent to Mexico. All were men who had given up the world to follow after Jesus in the manner that Francis of Assisi had done, a life of poverty and work for Jesus. Cortez turned the nation over to this small band of zealous workers, and they spread a simple gospel of the Lord Jesus Christ throughout Mexico.

In time, Rome overshadowed their work, but still the Promise of God they had sown lingered far back in the higher elevations of the rocky Sierra Madres.

The Spirit of God was evident on some of these Indians with their embroidered white pajama outfits and wide brimmed *sombreros.*

One of the Indians who had great problems adjusting to the bars and order of the prison was placed in my dorm. I don't know what people had told him about me, but he singled me out to vent his misery on. He would come in my cell and poke me up the behind, laugh and giggle, and run out. All this occurred in the early morning before I was awake. It was a rude awakening. One morning I was waiting for him. As soon as he crossed the doorway of my cell, I let him have it with a mop handle. He grabbed it, and then we locked in a titanic struggle over the mop handle.

I let him wear himself out and then wrested the mop handle from his hands. Down the hall he flew, with me and the mop handle in hot pursuit. I did not spare the rod.

Several days later, he started bleeding from the ears. It had nothing to do with the mop battle, but someone told him he had better leave the gringo alone. *(Psalm 105:13-15)* He turned to the Lord Jesus and found power in the name of the Almighty. He would creep up to a group of men sitting around talking and yell "Jesus!" The whole bunch would jump, and the Indian would break out laughing and walk away.

On the surface of the matter, it would seem to be an idiotic thing to do, but the man was running demons out of men by the power of God. Jesus uses the foolish things of this world to confound the wise. *(1 Corinthians 1:27)*

~~~~~~~~~~~~~~~~~

One day I watched as Edmundo (Edmundo was the man Toluca) took up a stand alongside a gate that required more that several hundred men to pass through on their way to a meeting, and within reach of Edmundo.

Edmundo was somewhat startled as the gates opened, and kids and men started moving past him at a fast pace. For lack of anything else to do, Edmundo started swatting each man on the back as they went by. After it was all over, he had 'laid hands' on a goodly part of the prison. Again, the foolishness of God. *(Acts 8:17, 1 Corinthians 1:27)*

Pecas was the strong leader of the young men who had come to Jesus in the prison. He was a very good soccer player and liked to dress.

I lived and slept in my rags and took a bath with my clothes on. I would fill a washtub full, sit in it, and stir around in the suds. In the very dry climate of Durango, it would take only a few minutes for me to dry out, clothes and all.

The clothes rack in Pecas' cell was bulging with some nice looking outfits. I told him that he had too much, considering the very meager circumstances of all those around us. "The Bible says if you have two coats, give one to those who have none." *(Luke 3:11)*

Pecas looked sideways with a strong questioning spirit, glanced a hard look off my head, thought deeply for a moment… then slowly and mournfully, unloaded his hoard. He loved Jesus. I thanked him and carried the large pile of clothes to the group of Indians from southern Durango.

I do not know what language they spoke, but somehow I got the point across using sign language and pieces of Spanish. I think there was a give and take of understanding in the Spirit.

In one very large area in southern Mexico, there are over two hundred languages spoken by the Indians, and many of these dialects are tonal. The meaning of the word can change with the tone of the voice. I was able to convey to the chief of the Indians the message that Pecas had given his clothes to them because of what Jesus had said. The chief got a very nice leather jacket.

Later, a fellow named Zapata fronted me and said he wanted the jacket. He said the chief was very rich and didn't need the jacket. "The chief has two cows and is very rich." There was nothing I could do about it, and the issue passed.

~~~~~~~~~~~~~~~~~

Matters within the high stone walls were relative. What would matter in the prison might not matter at all on the outside.

A friend of mine wanted to send me a thousand dollars. I sure appreciated the offer, but I told him that I could clean out a whole row of cells with the money, by paying for a release fee for many of the men. The ones I didn't help get out would hate me, and I would have to live with them. I didn't need this. If I placed the money in the bank at the prison, in time everyone would know about it, and the pressure upon me to help would attract more attention than I needed. Best I stay in my rags and eat what was put before me.

The operation of the gift of tongues, which Jesus had used in such a marvelous way on the streets of Durango, did operate on occasions in the prison. To my knowledge, Jesus has not used this gift to speak other languages since then. I still pray in tongues, and upon occasions speak in tongues and interpret *(1 Corinthians 14:27),* but I don't speak the language and bring forth messages as on the day of Pentecost. *(Acts 2:6-8)* Maybe before the Lord calls me home, He will grace my preaching once again as He did on the streets of Durango.

There were two horses that were allowed to roam the very large prison yard. At one end of the yard was a small farm that contained pigs, rabbits, chickens, and other animals. If you wanted a paintbrush, you went to one of the horses and snipped off whatever size you wanted from their manes or tails. The things had big, medium, and small brush cuts all over their manes and tails. I always felt some sort of kinship with the horses.

One morning the horses were not to be found. Then at dinner we had very large chunks of meat. It was the horses. Hungry as I was, I felt I would be eating the leg of a friend. I passed my meat on to someone who didn't claim kin to the horses.

When they killed the pigs, they would boil down a large amount of the fat until they had a big cauldron of boiling grease. They would then press the pig skin into the cauldron of boiling grease, causing the skin to bubble, making fried pork skins. They would cook up enough for hundreds of men to have a portion. I did not feel any kinship for the pigs, so I enjoyed eating a big stack of pork skins with Tabasco sauce.

~~~~~~~~~~~~~~~~~

Athletics took up a lot of time for the men, and the authorities saw to it that we got first class bats, balls, gloves, basketballs, or whatever we needed. The only thing the Americans couldn't get was an American football. Then that day rolled around when one real American football was brought into the prison and football, as it is played in the good old United States, was introduced to Durango.

Some of us went at it. We enlisted the soccer players, and it was first and ten. We played tackle, barefooted and with no pads in the rocky yard. This was too rough, so we went to flag football. The Mexicans thought it insanity to play such a game and get all beat up and knocked down. The physical contact didn't make much sense to them. Giving the idea a little thought, they may have been correct.

At times, the prison would sponsor a basketball tournament. Busloads of school kids from Durango would pour into the prison, and for several days it was basketball all day long. The basketball games were the highlight of all the sports. The prison team was one of the best in the area. The down side was that all games had to be played at home, and the all-star picks couldn't play in town at the All-Star games. Such is the life of talent behind bars.

~~~~~~~~~~~~~~~~~~

Fighting between the men wasn't a big deal, but the guards would stop a serious fight if they could. Usually the fighting was a struggle to express one's manhood. Rarely did I see anyone hurt, and fights were far and few between.

An 'us against them' spirit kept the contention between inmates at bay, but when a serious fight did come about, someone usually got hurt. The serious fights were no holds barred—biting, kicking, gouging, or grabbing whatever was handy.

One man had his lower lip bitten off by another fellow. This wouldn't have been so bad if the other fellow hadn't swallowed the bite. So, the man wasn't able to retrieve the bitten off lip. He sure had a hard time talking after that. He had been a big mouth before his loss.

The hot water for showers came from a bank of four or five water heaters at the end of each dorm. They were located outside on the wall of the shower room. When shower time came, some of the men would stoke the wood fires that heated the water pipes, and others would shower. When you finished with a shower, you then became a stoker and did your turn outside keeping the pipes hot.

One day I attempted to boil an egg in a can on the end of a coat hanger down in the fire. It wasn't long before the guard in charge got my coat hanger, egg, and can, and away I was carried to the office.

To me, things had gotten out of hand as far as tormenting the gringo. The Director came by as I was being arrested and saw my predicament. With a wave of his hand I was set free, can, egg, and all. There was no rule against cooking an egg in the hot water heater. Thank You Jesus, He made a way of escape. He sure kept His Almighty Hand on me. *(1 Corinthians 10:13)*

~~~~~~~~~~~~~~~~~~

The sunsets across the dry Sierra Madres were spectacular to say the least. I was in a hard place in a hard land, but the inner joy Jesus brought to my soul gave me a deep appreciation of the natural wonders that swirled over and around us.

Tornadoes, monsoon rain and winds, and the display upon the natural heavens did not go unnoticed. Many times, some of the men would gather to watch the brilliant display of colors and clouds at sunset over the mountains.

Brilliant hues of reds would flash across the sky, and then slowly fade as the sun dipped into the Pacific. These were events to us, and they cost nothing. Jesus would dip His finger in a paint and then, with broad, sharp, strokes, create something beautiful in the earthly heavens.

~~~~~~~~~~~~~~~~~~

The Americans seemed to enjoy tormenting me with their unbelief. They laughed at the Bible. They acted as if they were afraid of nothing, but when I started talking about death, it was another story. The inner man well knew what lay ahead after death, and of God's final judgments. *(Revelation 20:15, Ephesians 3:16)*

The carpenter shop was a very large tin building, and many different things were fabricated here. In one corner coffins were built; all sizes, large, medium, and small.

On occasions, the Americans would work at banging nails into the boxes of death. One day I came upon several Americans who thought they were very tough. A large coffin stood between us. I took the lid off the coffin, then slid down inside. I pulled the lid back on and lay there, as the small group of gringos looked on, bug-eyed.

A moment passed, and I began to laugh with my cackling, maniacal laugh. Then I opened the lid and stood up. They all still stood bug-eyed and startled beyond words as I walked away. They didn't have an answer for death.

~~~~~~~~~~~~~~~~~~

Many times Pecas and I would roam the halls of the prison at night before lockdown. It was like downtown in a crowded small town, with people going and coming—some working on wood projects, others gambling, and others standing around talking. Pecas had his guitar; he would play, and I would back him up the best I could with my whistling.

We would stay in one area for awhile, sing and preach, and then move on. It was street preaching at its best, and Pecas was good.

One night in another dorm, I was able to talk a short man with a ruddy complexion, who had an accordion, into going around and playing for me as I sang in tongues. Away we would go, up and down the halls. He'd fire up his accordion, which was about as big as he was. He didn't know the Christian hymns, but when he played *Under the Double Eagle*, my hair stood on ends.

He would play for hours all the songs he had learned playing in bars. He knew all the old Mexican favorites. At times I would just stand back and enjoy the spirit the man had on his music. After our short tour together, I never did see the man again.

Much of the work Jesus was doing was being done in the Spirit. Every now and then He would let me see a glimpse of what was going on, and this always made me redouble my efforts.

One young man who believed strongly in Jesus would always yell at me from out of a window or say to me in passing, "With Christ all things are possible!" *(Matthew 19:26)* How true he was.

~~~~~~~~~~~~~~~~~

Pecas, the young leader of the Christians in the prison, had an uncle in the prison. His crime was robbing the poor boxes at Catholic churches. I never did hear how he got caught, but he was no doubt tops in his profession. Somewhat small with black, curly hair, he was always quick with a smile, and seldom was there other than a smile on his face. He stood near the batter and was the prison cheerleader at the baseball games.

His job in the prison intelligence system was to listen to the conversations and orders from the Director's Office. Most of the guards considered him somewhat crazy and paid little attention to him. He would sit under the window of the Director's office and digest the information that he overheard, and he overheard everything.

One noon he came in, laughing, and told us of a heated conversation between the Director and some of his assistants. The assistants were trying their best to convince the Director that I was not insane, but a very bad person, and should be dealt with harshly. *Thank You, Jesus,* the Director held his stand for me.

The small group lived around me was proud of its information gathering. Most of the time we knew what the order of the day was before it reached the assistants. The men around me were first class intelligence agents, or better, first class spies.

~~~~~~~~~~~~~~~~~~

One morning, Joe, the young American in the prison for having a bag of marijuana, came running up with a small Bible in his hands. He was greatly excited. He said, "There is an American in the prison handing out hundreds of Bibles." We had prayed for Bibles and had been able to obtain a few, but Jesus had answered prayer, and a man had brought hundreds of the *Reina Valera* version in Spanish. This was some kind of breakthrough, and everyone in the prison obtained a free New Testament Bible.

Bill, the American who brought the Bibles, had a ministry of giving Bibles to the men in prisons over Mexico. On several occasions we talked at length, and he did his best to reach officials in Mexico to obtain my release. I lost track of Bill, but he sure helped while I was in the prison.

~~~~~~~~~~~~~~~~~~

Every day was a new show. I was in a spotlight. I lived in a fish bowl. Even when I made a sandwich from tuna in a can, two or three people would stop and watch me make my sandwich and continue to stare at me like a TV ad until I consumed the whole sandwich. I guess you pay a price for fame, or in my case, being infamous.

~~~~~~~~~~~~~~~~~~

Sunday, the home team was well along on, putting down one batter after the other and walking away with another win. It was serious business. I made my way up behind the visiting teams' bench. I had to pass it to get to the other side of the ball diamond. Everything was fine until one kid turned his head and saw me. He turned his head back and yelled, "Sherman!"

The visitors all turn their heads, and the next thing I know I am surrounded by all the members of the visiting team. They started asking questions, "Why did you knock over the statues," and, "Where do you live in the prison?" I didn't have any answers. About this time, one young man handed me a soda. I told him that Jesus had impressed upon me to tell him that one day he would be a great preacher. He agreed with my observation; he believed he would be a great preacher one day.

My interview didn't last long, as the small gathering attracted attention, and no one knew just what was going on. The alarms started going off and the special guards came running.

I was ordered off the area, and the visiting team was ordered back to their bench. I gave my only shirt to the young man who gave me a soda. Later he was unable to take the old shirt out of the prison, and it was returned to me.

I don't guess the confrontation at the ballgame was much of an event, but it greatly heartened me to know that my stand for Jesus Christ was not going unnoticed beyond the prison walls. Many people had turned their hearts to my message of Jesus, but I never met them. One day I am sure I will meet those whose heartfelt prayer in Christ strengthened and kept me. One day, what a day that will be, when my Jesus I do see.

~~~~~~~~~~~~~~~~~~

The tall, young Mexican with the long dangling arms stood in the corner of the small crowded house used by the inmates as a watering hole. It was the one place where you could find shelter from the ever-present authority of the prison. One could get a tortilla with beans and coffee for a few cents. The Americans had taught the inmates who ran the sandwich house how to make egg sandwiches. It wasn't McDonalds, but anyone could get a soda and a bite to eat any time during the day.

The tall Mexican had just come back from a hearing at the judicial section, and he was with the administrative guard who had escorted him. Everyone was in good spirits, and the small, crowded, one room house buzzed with laughter and small talk.

All the inmates knew the tall, young man was a notorious pickpocket and thief. He was a pro. I do believe evil, supernatural powers had control of his hands. They seemed to move without him being aware of it. He had a light, deft touch. Even the inmates placed a sure hand on their valuables when he came around.

The administrative guard smiled at everyone and enjoyed the moment of being one with the army of men who lived behind bars. He ordered for the young man in his care and himself. Then he reached for his wallet. No wallet! He slapped his pants pockets and patted his jacket pockets. No wallet! A strange look of bewilderment came over him.

About this time, some of the men near him began to laugh. They knew what had happened.

Then it dawned on the guard that somehow the young man with the dangling arms had taken his wallet. He turned, and with a small bit of anger, he grabbed the young man by the shirt and demanded his wallet. The man didn't even blink an eye as he handed over the wallet. The men around the room laughed, and the event passed.

Honor among thieves? I don't think so. Those hands of the young man would steal from another thief, or even his mother. He was out of control, or rather, under a very powerful control.

Spirits get hold of people. *(Mark 5:2)* One man was thrown in a solitary cell raging. The guards didn't want to hurt him and were able to get him locked up. They didn't have any strait jackets. Later some were made.

The man, with a supernatural strength, began to rip the cell plumbing and pipes out of the wall and throw them at the guards. The guards proceeded to shoot mace and tear gas at the enraged fellow. He licked the mace like soda pop and took in the tear gas like cigarette smoke.

This went on until the cell was totally demolished and the man, winded by his efforts of demolition, sat down and laughed. The guards didn't want to open the bars and take him on physically. They looked at each other, and one said, "He has a devil." How true were his words. Some time later I saw the man working around the prison. Much prayer had gone up for him, and it was only prayer that pulled him from hell. He looked and acted much better.

The weekends were like traffic at a busy airport. Long lines of waiting visitors and buses loaded and unloaded. Thousands of visitors poured in and out of the prison. A deep struggle was taking place in the spirit world. As the spiritual burdens of the visitors were being thrown on the spiritual fortress that the prison had become, spiritual powers in high places were being torn down. The Lord let me see this in a vision.

Durango had become the spiritual center of Mexico. God's people were holding forth. I thanked Jesus for allowing me to have part in the battle. Jesus was doing it all in the spirit, and outcome had not been placed in any man's hand. It didn't matter if I lived or died; Jesus was going to have His way. Jesus had a great love for His people in Durango and Mexico. The die had been cast.

A few years before, I sent some money to a missionary couple who traveled into Mexico. Over a period of time I had lost track of them. One day I happened upon a Bible in a desk in one of the shops where men learned various skills. In the Bible was a short note, and the date on which an American missionary had visited the prison and left the Bible. The name of the missionary was the name of the man I had sent money to several years before.

I often wondered who said the prayer to place

in motion the effort of the Almighty to lift the judgments from His people in Durango. Perhaps on Judgment Day all will be known.

The Indian heritage was evident in the face of the large prison guard, as he stood in reverence to the strains of the Mexican National Anthem. A tear worked its way out of an eye, and several more appeared. This was a tough guy and the tears came from the heart, from his love for his country. It was only for a moment, yet it was the expression of the true Mexican. What love for his country, and they played "that song" every day about the same time. The blessings of God, the blessings of God, they had been with holding. Cursed from the Rio Grande to the jungles of Guatemala, from the Pacific to the Caribbean. Cursed because a bunch of nuts with robes, white collars, candles, and a hundred ways to reach the Almighty held such wonderful people in forced spiritual slavery.

Only a moment of expression, yet a moment that reached across a span of centuries from that brutal day at Calvary, when liberation for God's people in Mexico had been paid for. No 'maybes', no 'ifs', and no 'buts'. I could sense in my soul the stirring winds of an eternal Spirit, even now moving across a nation, to and fro, selecting those destined for eternal life and also the blessings in this life. Jesus was moving, and my efforts were on the winning side.

I thought I had come to help Mexico, but

maybe Mexico was helping old Roberto. The Apostle Paul said in one missionary journey they found a group of people who had a law of love among themselves. I think it could be said of the Mexicans that they had this law also.

One fellow who had constantly vented abuse upon me in different ways was warned by the Spirit of God that if he did not change his ways, repent, and turn to righteousness, he would be dead in three days.

I felt the anointing of the Lord Jesus Christ as I leveled my arm and hand toward him. "Three more days to live if you don't repent and turn to Jesus." He looked at me somewhat doubtfully as I turned and walked away.

The next day around noon, he staggered from his cell in a semi-paralytic state. Something had happened to his body functions, and he could hardly stand up.

As he leaned against the doorpost of the gate which opened into the dusty yard, I passed by and saw the fear in his eyes, and the pitiful shape of his body.

Maybe I should have tried to show him mercy and comfort, but it wasn't in me at the time to do so. Of all things, I started to laugh at him. Then I started digging a hole in front of him in the rocky dry soil. With such a laugh I cackled and said, "Tomorrow we are going to put you in the ground, you are a dead man, ha, ha, ha." He turned, and as best he could, fled to the safety of his cell. *The gringo is a mad man,* he must have thought.

A funny thing about the 'tomorrow' message was, a number of the men looking on all nodded their head and seconded the message, "For sure you are dead."

That night, with great effort the man made his way to me. Shaking and just barely able to talk, he said, "I repent and accept Jesus as my Savior." Then, to salvage a little of the great pride he had lost, he said, "Do you repent also?"

"Yes," I laughed, "I repent also."

The next day he was up and going as if nothing had happened, but it had. Down deep in his soul there had been a true change.

Some come by fear and others come by love. *(Jude 1:22,23)* The love message didn't work here, but fear was a sure winner.

Never did I care to see anyone hurt or see anyone claimed by death, but let's get very real about Holy Scripture. Paul spoke of his power of sharpness not to harm anyone but to help them. *(2 Corinthians 13:10)* He also told one church that they were to cause one man to be put to death by Satan to save his spirit on the Day of Judgment. *(1 Corinthians 5:5, Revelation 20:11-13)* Death of the body is one thing and the death of a soul is another. *(Matthew 10:28)* Paul also mentioned that he delivered two men to Satan to teach them a lesson. *(1 Timothy 1:20)*

At one time in my life, a well-meaning prayer group decided that I was well beyond help and needed to be put in the hands of Satan to cease my suffering. They warned me, and sure enough, one fine afternoon Satan answered their prayer. He stood in the air at a good distance from me brandishing his large sword of death. The only problem he had was that a legion of beautiful powerful angels quick-timed between us. They veiled themselves; they didn't want to look at him. With mighty swords raised, they shot fire from their swords upon him.

This turned the oncoming force of death, and Satan backed away to a comfortable distance. Then he came again. This time I started speaking in tongues, and a vision of Jesus appeared before me. I could see that the words I was speaking were not mine, but those of our Lord. The words spoken by the gift of tongues caused Satan to exit the area in great fear. The interpretation of the tongues being spoken was clear; "Get away from My son." *(1 Corinthians 12)*

True, the angels had great power, but the words spoken by the Almighty sealed Satan away from me that day.

The warfare in the spiritual world is a very silent, real, and forceful thing. Jesus gives His people the power to rise up and smite the forces that would harm them. All power was given to Him. *(Matthew 28:18)*

No one has any power except Jesus, and as brothers and members of the Family of God, we share a part of His power. He gives us the power we need at the time we need it.

One needs to ask for an increase in faith and step out into the supernatural with a sweet soul by faith. The Lord will meet you where your faith is. Ask and you shall receive. *(Matthew 7:7)* Ask for guidance if you get in the wrong place or make mistakes. Keep mercy, grace, and kindness over your spirit, and Jesus will get you through.

The prayer group that ordered Satan to destroy me felt they were doing the proper thing, but their prayer was not in the will of God. *(1 John 5:14)* Another spirit hovered nearby and influenced their prayer.

My speaking death to the man was in the will of God and ordered by God. *(1 Corinthians 5:5)* It was His Word, and it did not come back void. *(Isaiah 55:11)*

In time a great change came over the man, and he was strength to my efforts in a hard land. Had not I warned, I would have been the one who would have been put in the ground three days later. *(Ezekiel 3:18)*

Chivo was a small skinny man, with large brown soulful eyes. I never did find out why he was in prison. Chivo feared no man, but he did fear God. *(Psalms 115:13)* On one occasion, he had a standoff with Paco. Harsh words were passed back and forth, and little Chivo rose up against the tiger of the prison. "Come on, come on," he shouted at Paco with an intense force. Chivo won the shouting match, as Paco did not 'come on.'

On occasions he would get drunk on whiskey. He would stagger around the prison yard until one of the guards picked him up. I never knew how he got the whiskey into the prison, and even a very intense investigation by the authorities never turned up anything.

We all thought Chivo must have had a special bottle placed in the soft drink truck on the outside, and then carted through the gates with the other sodas.

When I left the prison, Chivo had pretty well gone off the deep end with whiskey and drugs. Somehow, even if he were locked up in segregation, he would end up with a few joints of marijuana. The guards couldn't watch everyone all the time. Even visiting girlfriends and wives would smuggle drugs into the prison beneath their clothes.

The one thing that stayed on the minds of every inmate in the prison was the day they would get out of prison. Some of the men had stored information in their minds about the comings and goings of the guards down to seconds. They watched day and night, week on end, month on end, and year on end. They knew who slept, what time they awoke, and what they did.

On occasion the guards would do things to

break the pattern, but the dogged determination of some of the prison smarts would always come back, and in short time they had the routine of the prison patterned.

Every now and then, a man would see an opening and make a break for it. While I was there, I knew of only one failed escape and of several successful escapes.

Two men who were later to beat Rojo's head in with lead pipes, made a try at the wall near the segregation section.

The sun was just fading over the mountains when they got halfway up the wall. Several volleys of shots from the guards ended the ill-timed effort. Both fell to the ground. Neither had been hit, but the fall knocked the wind out of them.

As long as you didn't use force in your escape effort, you received a very light punishment if you didn't make it. Using force was a different matter.

The sun had not come up one morning, and the men milled around in semidarkness waiting for the morning exercises to begin. Two men had charted their escape days before, and that morning the opportunity presented itself.

In the breaking cool dawn, they could see no heads in the nearest watchtower. They knew the guards were asleep.

Days before, they had plotted their course up over a small building, across the large garden, up onto the scaffolding workers were using to work on the high outside wall, and finally, a long drop, and they were free.

The plan worked, and the men were never seen again. It was a blessing to those left, as the morning exercises were cancelled.

I had been standing in an upstairs window singing in tongues. *(1 Corinthians 14:15)* One guard passed by downstairs and pointed at me. He laughed so hard and long that he fell to the ground, and then he continued to laugh and roll from one side to the other. I didn't know I was that funny. The next day he was in a cell on the row below me, behind bars, with a big lock.

He had been escorting a group of men working in the fields. When he returned, he was one man short, and didn't know where he lost him. The order of the day was that the guard had to finish the term of the sentence. In most cases there was a way made whereby the guard could obtain his release.

I went by the cell, and there was my laughing friend. I said, "Much ha, ha, ha." He knew he had asked for it. He looked at his feet in a very humble and dejected manner and said, "No ha, ha, ha." He was soon released, but he lost his job. Later he visited the prison as a member of a visiting baseball team. It was good to see him. On his uniform was the number five. "The Lord has given you grace," I said.

He smiled and said, "Yes, God has given me

grace."

The last escape while I was there was out through a low spot in the wall. Two drug dealers were said to have made a payoff for someone to look the other way. Whether they did or didn't make a payoff, the two fellows made it out. One was later caught drunk downtown and brought back to the prison.

With much extra time to dream up escape plans, some of the Americans would hatch one plan after the other: from digging out, to rigging a hang glider and going off a building roof on a very windy day.

The guards didn't like to see the Americans congregate near any gate. Few understood English and, not knowing what was being said or planned, assumed that it presented a threat of escape, whether true or not.

One fellow in a prison in Mexico City paid for a helicopter to land in the prison yard and pick him up. He made it out and to the United States.

I do believe the men God had His Hand on would have found it impossible to escape, unless Jesus wanted them to do so. The Angels of God didn't take naps.

~~~~~~~~~~~~~~~~~

One of the prophecies given me before I came to Mexico was that a woman would be brought to me for prayer. She would be in a deranged mental state, and her dress would be torn under the arm on one side.

In my own mind, I had envisioned the woman and the situation. It didn't turn out as I had pictured it. For some reason, (I don't remember just why), a number of other men and I were ordered to the clinic for shots or blood tests, or something like that.

Next to the clinic was the women's prison. While we were seated in the large waiting room, a group of young girls were brought over from the women's prison.

One girl rushed to the desk in the waiting room and grabbed the list of men to be called to the clinic. In an off-handed manner she spoke to me, "Hi, Sherman," and proceeded to *ooh* and *ah* over the list of men. Then she proceeded to expound on the manly virtues of her male friends whose names she saw on the list. It was the opening of a small circus. Other girls looked at the list, but none could compete with the noises and vocalizing of the first girl.

One young lady started around the room cracking the knuckles of all seated. She would request your hand and then crack your knuckles.

For lack of anything else to do, I extended my knuckles to be cracked when asked. The girl took my hand, and as she did, I prayed for her. There in front of me was a girl with a rip in her dress, and the Lord spoke to me—this was the woman of the prophecy.

She let out a faint gasp as the evil spirit went out of her, and then her face flushed and she took on a new countenance.

The devil which had bound her mind was gone, and she became a new person. What I had been told months before had come to pass.

All the prophecies that had been given to me had now come to pass, except the one of me returning to the United States.

The first event of prophecy was, I would be held up at the border for a day before entering Mexico. This had come to pass. Meeting the mob of students in the streets of Durango had also come to pass, as Jesus had shown by His foreknowledge.

The woman was the third event. Needless to say, I did have a great problem on my hands, as had been foretold in the fourth prophecy, and now I awaited the second part of that event to come about- getting back to the United States safely.

~~~~~~~~~~~~~~~~~

One letter I received while in prison was pretty rough. A friend of many years, who had found a heart to help me buy gas and supplies to get to Mexico, wrote in somewhat harsh words that he wasn't my friend anymore.

He had no idea or understanding of what was

going on, but his wife was Catholic. Somehow, the parting of the friend didn't matter all that much, and I felt that one day he might come to an understanding of the truth. Other letters came over the months. Most had a few dollars, and this was appreciated. The group that had stood so strong with me in spiritual support tried at times to get various articles through the mail to me, but often they were sent back because of money due on customs importation regulations.

I found it very hard to convey my feelings and situation to anyone. To remain halfway sane, I tuned the world out and lived within my circumstances.

Anyone who has been in prison for any length of time can understand this. The Lord had work for me to do, and He wanted this work done. With all the spiritual pressures that had been and were now coming against me, I doubt if I would have been able to stay in Mexico and complete His work, had I not been in the prison.

Outside of the physical hardships one encounters in the mission field (and these can be harsh but bearable), the great battle that is fought is in the spirit over a person's will and mind. This is where the missionary wins or loses. The Bible speaks of a cloak of zeal. *(Isaiah 59:17)* Without this cloak of zeal, evil powers can put to flight well-meaning people. I suffered a battering in the spirit, and had I been left to my own way I would have no doubt flown to other places. Jesus took care of this problem with the high wall and the guards, and the Mexican law.

Little by little the outside world faded, and the very real circumstances I found myself involved in came into a clear focus.

Whether people hated me, or whatever people thought of me one way or the other, didn't really matter. What mattered was right in front of me. My world was right in front of me, and in a sense, I died to the outside. It was a slow protracted death.

I thought the first thing I would do when I got out would be to buy a hamburger. For someone who had never tasted of McDonalds or Burger King, this desire would have never come about. A lot died within me, but I never died out to hamburgers.

~~~~~~~~~~~~~~~~~

The Durango area had a former and latter rain. The former rain would start the crops, and later, the latter rain would bring the crops in. If either one failed, it meant suffering.

Within the prison walls was a very large garden, and it was worked by the men of the prison. One day at dinner, after clear evidence that the former rains were upon us, the large group of garden workers turned toward where I was seated. With mock uplifted hand, they all gave thanks to the saints and laughed at me. It didn't rain again for six months, and the crops failed. From time to time, I would openly mock this group, and loudly cackle at them with my maniacal laugh. *(1 Kings 18:27)* Jesus was having His day.

I had never experienced such strong spiritual powers as I did in the confines of the Durango Social Rehabilitation Center (the prison). Along with the high arm of Jesus *(Jeremiah 27:5),* the rod given Moses was being thrown in the court. The legions of Rome had faith, but the rod of Moses was devouring their faith. One was gaining power and the other was losing. No fire from Heaven had come down to smite Sherman. All watched from the sideline. The whole struggle was no small matter anymore. The Word of God was being preached in a more evident way. The words of Psalm 140 had become a harsh reality both inside and outside of the prison.

Several times Jesus would let me see the large blinding ball of fire He stood in overhead, with His forehead low and arm stretched forth. As I walked in the prison yard, He would guard me high overhead. Evil powers would loom across horizon, and Jesus would wheel and set His arm. That would put an end to problems.

My faith was on a roll.

Chapter Ten

Who Sent You to Mexico?

And Asa did that which was good and right in the eyes of the Lord his God: For he took away the altars of the strange gods, and the high places, and brake down the images... 2 Chronicles 14:2,3

The anointing of Jesus that had stood with me in such a wondrous and powerful way on the streets of Durango had now returned, and it seemed much greater. With God's faith and power came a fearlessness and boldness. No mistake about it; the anointing of Jesus was an awesome force. All things were possible as long as I did and asked in the will of God. The laws of the natural world were overcome by God's eternal power. The blind do see, the lame do walk, the deaf do hear, and the dead are brought back to life.

Our Almighty God is able to do anything. I felt no one could touch my soul. I did know my flesh could be touched if it was the Will of God. I also knew my will should match up with the Will of God in my prayer. *(James 4:15)* Not by force or might did the Almighty choose to save people, but by the foolishness of preaching. *(1 Corinthians 1:21)* In my case, if anything was done in a great spiritual sense, it had to be God. These people lived with me in a very transparent world.

Had we been a large group, the group would have gotten the glory and not The Almighty. Jesus could show forth His power around Sherman and no one would question the matter. Sherman was a puddle of puke, half-nuts and wild-eyed, but the nutty, wild-eyed puddle of puke was on a roll behind Jesus.

Whatever had happened to the common grace of the people of the Catholic Church I didn't know. I did know there was no longer a spiritual cover protecting them. The gates of hell were boiling and thrusting outward. Nearness to small Catholic shrines made me sick, and sores were breaking out on the men in the prison.

I took two large sheets of plywood, painted them white, and in red letters wrote the Ten Commandments. I went throughout the prison and threw the entire host of small, Catholic altars and shrines in the trashcans. Then I left the two large boards where all could see them. No one said anything to me, but the young kids who had been saved in the prison and had formed a strong force, were escorted to one of the offices. Before their fearful eyes the pieces of plywood were smashed, and I was labeled a mad man. The score was tied and the bases were loaded, and it was late in the game.

The following Sunday, the *Padre* arrived and set up shop in the dining room of my dorm. I began to itch all over, and my head throbbed. A plague was on. Don't try to convince me that the spiritual anointing of Rome wasn't the cause.

It became apparent that the agent of Rome had faith he could confront me in my very own dining room. I had not asked for this moment. The entire matter was being thrust upon me. Such a great evil was now upon me with great power. If a confrontation was what Rome demanded, then I would have my say.

The man with all the robes and candles was holding forth. I started into the dining room to have my say. All his robes and holy water didn't faze me. Then I stopped. A thought came to me that this wouldn't be the right thing to do. The itching got worse. I grabbed my Bible, and, waving it high overhead, started yelling in tongues, and into the most Holy Communion I went. Yelling and waving my Bible, I marched around the front of the group. Wide-eyed, the *Padre* stood speechless. I knew all the men. We ate at the tables where this 'thing' was being held. I marched up and down alongside the tables. One man made a move to stand between the *Padre* and me. The other men looked on in wonder. I could get no reaction, but I was having 'my say'.

No one moved. I backed away from the group and backed into a life-sized, china statue of a man on a cross. I know they all said it was Jesus, but this fellow didn't look like the Jesus I knew, and he had a large sheet wrapped around him. Anyone who had read the Bible knew the soldiers gambled among themselves for His garments and hung my Father up like a side of beef on a slaughterhouse with nothing covering the flesh. It wasn't a pretty sight. Rome did this, and here they were again. My hand went up, and over the false Christ went. In the silence of the moment, it was a crash that was heard in Heaven.

My friends on the benches in front of me came alive like hornets having their nest shaken by a bear. It was their turn to holler and yell, and as they charged me, the dam broke. When they came within arm's length, I took my Bible, and with both hands I started swinging. One good blow from the anointed Bible sent men sailing to one side or the other. A spiritual wall came around me, and the group that charged me stood outside yelling and shaking their fists. They were having 'their say'. The *Padre* yelled and tried to calm the uproar, but nothing doing. An "imagination" had been smashed.

As far as I am concerned, a person can have all the statues they want, and as long as they don't get in the way of God's two great laws, no harm is done. You start talking to those wooden or stone monkeys, and they become your God.

When Jesus came, He brought a fulfilling of the Mosaic Law and Commandments. *(Matthew 5:17)* The commandments He had given Moses were no longer good enough. When Jesus came, He gave us a law of the heart. When asked, *"Which is the great commandment in the law?"* Jesus answered, *"Thou shalt love the Lord thy God with all thy heart, and with all thy soul, and with all thy mind. This is the first and great commandment."* (Matthew 22:36-38)

The Spirit we define as God or Lord has a name, a *"name which is above every name..."* and *"every tongue should confess that Jesus Christ is Lord." Philippians 2:9,11*

The Bible tells us the object of all our love should be The Spirit of The Lord Jesus Christ. *(Philippians 2:10)* The crucifix can be used as a reminder of the suffering the Man Jesus went through for us, or it can become more than a reminder. Wood or plaster can become a sacred object in someone's mind. The crucifix is a powerful reminder, nothing more, nothing less.

Jesus is all Truth, and we are to set our sights on Truth, loving that which is true with all our heart, soul, and mind. *(Matthew 22:37)* Worship is making a personal statement of one's feelings of and to the One True Almighty God, Whom we know at this time as The Lord Jesus Christ. It can be done in a number of ways.

"And the second is like unto it, Thou shalt love thy neighbor as thyself. On these two commandments hang all the law and the prophets." Matthew 22:40

Those powerful, enduring, divinely-inspired words from the pen of the little man from Tarsus to the churches of the Galatians echo and follow the perversion of God's Holy Word down through the ages– *"But though we, or an angel from heaven, preach any other gospel unto you than that which we have preached unto you, let him be accursed. As we said before, so say I now again, If any man preach any other gospel unto you than that ye have received, let him be accursed."* Galatians 1:8,9

The pure Word of God tells us there is only one way to reach the Almighty God, through the Man, Jesus Christ. Paul wrote to Timothy and told him the only way to the Almighty was through Christ Jesus. *"For there is one God, and one mediator between God and men, the man Christ Jesus;"* 1 Timothy 2:5

The Almighty God in His Holy Word said the only one to pray to is Christ Jesus. To pervert God's Word and tell people you can call upon the blessed woman who brought Jesus into this world or any of His disciples is a gross perversion, and the curse Paul spoke of follows with a heavy hand. Paul said even if a true man of God, an angel, a messenger, or an angelic vision from heaven came and spoke words that conflicted with his Divinely inspired words, they would be accursed. *(Galatians 1:8,9)*

How right and correct a person must be regarding the preaching of the True Gospel of Jesus Christ. *(James 3:1)* The punishment in this world is harsh, but in the hereafter there is no recourse. You go to heaven or to hell, and if you find yourself in hell, you'll stay there until the Day of Judgment. Don't be fooled into thinking someone will pray you out. *"...it is appointed unto men once to die, but after this the judgment." Hebrews 9:27*

What was done was done. Later I would go to the Director and tell him I repented of my efforts to preach in the prison, and I would pay for the broken statue. It seemed no one understood, but the itch left with the broken pieces of china. Wood, metal, or stone, it was all deaf and dumb.

The riot alarms went off all over the prison. Guards came running with their cans of mace and tear gas. The leader of the squad pointed his can at me, but did not turn it loose.

I pointed my finger at him and told him if he bothered me, he would be in bad trouble. Such audacity by the gringo! I meant what I said, and the guard heeded me. In the coming days, his wisdom in not blasting me with mace saved his job. I was escorted to the main office.

Leaving the building, I passed a small group of men who had been to a Pentecostal-type of meeting. They had no idea what had just transpired and began to shout in jest, "No more images." This upset the guards, for it seemed Belfast had crossed the ocean to the prison. We passed through one gate, and I ran head on into the visiting Pentecostal pastor. His arms were laden with statues of praying hands. He was visibly shaken as I was shoved past him, escorted by a squad of serious, unsmiling guards. The air crackled with tension. It was a beautiful Sunday, but no one cared or noticed.

As I have written before, the statues were not the issue. The way of Rome was the issue, and the itch was the issue. All the sin they told people they were going to talk to God about and get rid of didn't go anywhere. It stayed on their heads and the heads of those who followed them. God didn't get their messages.

"Oh, woe is me," I thought. The young officer I considered a friend was caught in a situation not at all to his liking. I felt they all knew I wasn't violent or dangerous, but this statue incident was destroying the peace and order of the prison. We were at a point where someone might get hurt or killed. They worked hard at running a tight ship, and now I had become a first class problem.

I was locked in a cell on the upper deck. The mood wasn't friendly, and in any other place and with some other people, I might have been shot that night.

I was past the point of being talked to or reasoned with. The silence of the guards troubled me a bit. Again doubt pounded on my head. Perhaps I was crazy. What in the world was I doing here?

The lockdown came. No one said anything, but I felt something was up. Then, two guards came and escorted me to the main office. I was told to go into a certain room and wait. Before long, a group of guards came in, led by a man who I had thought was my friend. With him was the guard who heeded my warning about not shooting me with his mace can. He protested that I was a man of God, and he wasn't going to shoot a man of God. The group of guards stood at a distance, and my friend questioned me.

"Who sent you to Mexico?" he asked. I replied, Jesus had sent me to Mexico, and I was in Mexico because of God's Word. He sneered, "The Bible", and with those words, the anointing of God manifested.

Jesus was still with me. This time they unloaded their mace and tear gas. They blinded me, but throughout the whole melee, I could see everything. A large devil had fallen over my friend, and a black spiritual cloud overhead hyped the other guards.

At this point, Jesus yelled at me with a strong voice, "Lay no charge." *(Acts 7:60)* I started receiving blows and kicks from all sides. I heard my friend say they were not to hit me in the face. The kicks and blows continued, and I stood there. The Holy Spirit gave me a supernatural power to stand. I didn't feel the blows, although some were quite severe. They banged and kicked away at me.

Then Jesus told me, "Fall down." Down I went! With that act, all the men ran out of the room. I sat watching everything, and it was comical. A minute or so later, they stuck their heads into the doorway to see if I was hurt. It was bewildering. These men didn't want to hurt me. They had been pushed. I told them I was all right, and there was no charge on my part.

I was escorted back to my cell. There, I underwent a far greater beating in the spirit as hell crawled up through the slime pits and raised its voice in a spiritual manner. The sword of division was once again cutting to the quick.

The Catholic press once again came to life. Sherman had done it this time. Not only had he attacked the Queen of Heaven, but now he had turned on her son.

I was locked up. I fasted and prayed. Before going to Mexico, I had fasted as long as 40 days. I didn't have to worry; no food was served to me. I am sure I would have been forgiven and released if I told them I was sorry for my actions. I didn't, so, we all hung tough. Ten days went by, and no food. I could have cared less, but others were pretty upset. You either ate or you died.

About this same time, the Americans in prison in Mexico City went on a hunger strike to protest the conditions they had to live under. The fasting made the news, and political pressure was stirred from the north of the Rio Grande. Word reached the Director of the fasting in Mexico City and my *fasting* in the prison. I was called in and asked why I wasn't eating. Somehow, I avoided the issue and was released and sent back to my dorm.

Pressure was heavy on the prison authorities to do something about the gringo. They had beaten, kicked, and starved me; about all that was left was to shoot me. I watched everything with an inner assurance that at the proper time Jesus would move if I were in danger.

~~~~~~~~~~~~~~~~~

I felt there were strong measures being taken to have me done away with. In their eyes, I wasn't just a crazy nut anymore. I was first class trouble for the nation of Rome, and a perceived threat to the order of the prison. The Lord led me into a deeper walk in prayer and fighting spirits. Here in the silent spiritual world was the battleground for the souls of men. I was being forced deeper and deeper to keep my own soul.

I went around the prison doing my best to tell everyone to obey the laws and rules of the prison. There was no reason for 'Belfast' to find its way into our lives.

This quieted the authorities and took pressure off the guards. I really don't think there was as big a problem as they thought.

The matter was far from over. A toehold had been gained in the prison by forces on the outside, and once again the media vilified the hated gringo, Roberto. Before this, an article in a Durango newspaper said I had been seen about forty miles north of Durango, standing on a street corner as statues were thrown down in a Roman Catholic Church there. True or not, the statue bashing was no longer funny to the prison authorities. People were dying and being killed for various reasons, and the blame was coming to rest on my head.

I was tagged as a witch doctor, and about the only way some people knew how to handle a witch doctor was to kill him.

Several times I was on my way out of the prison. Just where to, I am not sure, but it was not an uncommon thing for people to be shot in custody for trying to escape. Each time Jesus moved, and I never made it out the front door.

A lawyer who had been engaged in trying to obtain farmland for the poor was shot after being picked up by special police. It was said, he had struggled with the police and was shot in front of the head during the struggle and killed.

After his burial, newspaper writers dug his body up and cut his skull in half with a skill saw. The cut was down the path of the bullet. There was no problem in seeing the path of the bullet and the furrows it made through the fellow's brain. In the life size photos, which were printed in the newspaper, it was very clear he had been shot in the back of the head.

I am sure these things happen in places around the world, but I was in a bad place for such to be going on. The special policemen were placed in the prison as a result of the article, and later transferred to Mexico City.

~~~~~~~~~~~~~~~~~

Ramon shuffled his way to his cell. Ramon was possibly the oldest man in the prison, and he and Sherman were of a handful of old timers in the place. Most of the men could find their way out of the prison, one way or the other, after a couple of years. Ramon was a jewel thief. Just whose jewels he stole I didn't know, but whoever he stole from offered him no mercy. Bent slightly with age and going blind, he made his way from a late shift job to the cell that he shared with Mudo and a newcomer, Sherman.

Sherman had been released from his *cut him no slack* cell; he was placed in a cell with Mudo and Ramon. Mudo had a harelip and couldn't speak very well, but he had a heart of gold and he bubbled with an inner joy.

Sherman was placed on the top bunk, a very strong cement slab extending from the wall. It wasn't hard for Sherman to see the wall over Ramon's bed, which was bedecked with icons and pictures of saints. A thin, gray cloud covered each picture. Sherman then knew the reason for Ramon's blindness; his drawing near to worship these pictures and figures on dumb wood covered with a spiritual blessing of the wrong kind.

Sherman had been beaten, starved, tormented, and everyone felt he had learned his lesson. This wasn't so; the war raged on in front of him and in his prison home. Mudo watched as, one by one, Sherman took the icons and pictures down and placed them under Ramon's slab. The crazy man still had fight in him.

It wasn't long before Ramon entered the cell, and in the darkness sought the objects of his worship. His hands moved across the face of the wall. It couldn't be; everything was gone. With a muffled scream he arose from his slab. It didn't take a wise man to figure out what had happened. Ramon staggered to the cell door screaming that Sherman had again attacked the Holy Images.

Sherman tried to calm him and explain why he was going blind. Ramon's eyes turned to Sherman in terror. The mad gringo was locked in his cell. What was going to happen next? Amid screams and shouts for the guards, Sherman tried to calm him, but to no avail: he could not forestall the midnight cry of Ramon's loss.

Guards came running, the lights went on, and the sirens were blaring forth. Mudo was in convulsions with laughter. Sherman tried to explain to the head security officer about the icons and Ramon's blindness. No one wanted to hear, and no one cared. Sherman had come to life again, and this meant trouble to the security officer on duty.

Sherman was escorted away from the screams and cries of Ramon and put in a separate cell alone.

The prison was in a state of change. The present Director was finishing his tour of duty with one foot out the door and wasn't looking back, and a new Director stood in the wings.

There was very little authority present from the top to deal with Sherman. Tight orders were given about dealing with the Americans. They were not to be beaten, as the American Consul made its rounds every now and then; the Mexicans did want good relations with the Americans. But then there was Sherman, and in the changing of the guard, a small group felt Sherman had crossed an unwritten line.

What was to be done with this troublemaker?

Not only had Sherman crossed an unwritten line, but also the small group of guards, by taking an unlicensed authority in the prison, had walked into a trap of their own making. Sherman could rat on them, and they could be put in the next cell.

Sherman had laid no charge, and as far as he was concerned, the matter was over. The unknown and guilty conscience worked an urgency on the rising outlaw group of guards. The guards thought it best to get Sherman before Sherman got them. There was no point in trying to explain to them that all was forgotten.

The best thing to do was to get Sherman out of the prison door in a very legal way and let him be torn by the dogs that awaited his exit.

Years before in Atlanta, Georgia, I had watched in questioning silence as a large squad of police awaited the exit of a man who had killed one of *their own.*

A traffic ticket had escalated into an intense shoot out in a large, vacant, three-story apartment house. An elderly policeman had been gunned down and the gunman chased into the apartment house. Then it was like using a hammer to kill a flea. Tear gas from all sides rocketed the building. After what seemed like an hour, though possibly it was only fifteen minutes, the cry went up, "Here he comes!"

The large crowd, which had gathered, moved back as a door opened at the top story of the building. Yes, the man was coming out, half blinded by the tear gas, but with no weapon and his hands in the air. In warfare, horrible things happen, but this was Atlanta, Georgia in broad daylight with a big crowd watching, and this man had his hands in the air. He was a very fat man and must have pushed the scales at three hundred pounds.

He stood in the open doorway at the top of a long outside staircase, with his hands in the air. A cry went up, "Shoot him!" and mercy fled the scene. No mercy was being offered that day. It sounded as if it was the Fourth of July and strings of firecrackers were being set off, as squads of police strained to empty their pistols and shotguns at the fat man. The man staggered back, and then sat down on the top steps with blood starting to ooze from his hits. He didn't make it to the hospital alive. I thought about all this, and the tales I had heard of treatment of the American drug dealers.

One man had been plucked from his small airplane and told to walk. He reared up and said, "No, sir, shoot me in the front." The police aimed their pistols and let loose several rounds near the man's ears. They laughed and threw him in the police wagon alive.

I felt once I was beyond the prison doors, I might be treated like the fat man. Jesus was going to have to move against this small group of men bent on getting me out the front door. I was sure that more than one of these men had the calling of God on their lives, and Satan was doing everything he could to get us all against the wall.

Saul of Tarsus had been pressed by Satan to not only destroy the Christians, but himself also. But the black cloud of Stephen's death did not come to rest upon Saul, later Paul, the great man of letters in the Holy Bible. Saul was shielded by Stephen's plea of *no charge. (Acts 7:60)*

I was in a dilemma as to what to do. I had picked up a saying that *If you don't know for sure what to do, then do nothing.* I also remembered a saying from my days in sports: *If you don't know what to do, do something, and for sure the other side will not know what you are doing.* I decided upon the former as opposed to the latter advice. If Jesus wanted me to do something, He would tell me. If not, then I would do nothing until hearing from the Master. I was now placed in a cell alone at the end of a long corridor of some fifteen cells.

Some people thought it was a good deal to live with the gringo. Others, like Ramon, froze in terror at the thought of being locked in a cage with the wild man.

You had to be careful about who you were locked up in a cage with all night. People would do strange things and not know what they had done the next day. People who liked to kill people could kill someone in the bunk under them, then go back to sleep until awakened by the guards investigating the murder.

I liked the idea of living in a single cell alone. There weren't enough cells for everyone to have his own cage.

To forestall anyone from moving in with me, I flooded the cell with water, then tore a cardboard box into small pieces and scattered it around the cell. I chewed all the garlic I could get a hold of. I smelled like an unwashed billy goat, breathed garlic, and made strange noises.

I am sure the real estate value of the nearby cells went down when I moved in, but no one selected me to live with.

Having the domestic issue somewhat under control, I didn't have to wait long before the escalating war with the renegade group of guards surfaced in a dramatic way.

No one was going to let the issue be. I had now become more of a threat than ever. I was enjoying the peace that the end of the road cell bought me, until one morning the security officer who led the rogue group of guards walked all the way down the long corridor to my cell.

This time he did not have his accompanying squad of guards. He wasn't popular, but the force he displayed did bring respect.

He was alone and moved fast. Sometimes some of the men carried a spike on a cob handle, or a small knife. In a matter of seconds, you could get a blade between the ribs and maybe not know who did it.

He came to my cell, gave me a fish-eyed small wave of the hand, and departed. Something had to be up. I pondered the moment. My home was being cased.

I do believe Jesus has given the nations of the world laws and government. *(Romans 13:1)* The Bible says the police are ministers of God to bring terror upon the ungodly. *(Romans 13:4)*

One guard asked if he could pray to Jesus. He had been told by the priest that his prayers had to be given to a priest before God would hear them. I told him "No, sir", he was a minister of God himself. I pointed out the scripture in Romans 13:4, *"for he is the minister of God"*.

The guard took on a new life when he read this scripture.

Not knowing the true ways of God's law, the rogue group of guards had stepped away from their spiritual franchise; the power and protection the law gave them. There was ample law in the prison to punish me and keep me under control, even if I bashed the statues over. They had locks and cages to keep the unruly in place. The problem was, they let the crazy priest turn the prison into their very own magical kingdom. We were a seemingly helpless lot, the ones who didn't bow the knee.

The noonday meal came and passed. Workers drifted in from the fields or where they worked in the prison.

That afternoon, soon after the security officer had given me the fish-eyed wave, another guard came by to tell me I had to move to another cell. There was no list made of the cell numbers of the new move. Maybe tomorrow they would get around to it.

I was moved into an area of tightly packed cells. Most of the men in this new area were killers of some sort. Spirits of terror swirled around these fellows. Most had a naturally fierce spirit, and the added hype in the spirit of their profession made them characters to be avoided.

After supper and before lockdown, they would line the hall and gamble by pinching pennies or throwing for a line. They cursed, gambled, and sang up until the lockdown time.

I lay on my new slab of cement amid the rags I kept along the side to deep me from falling. There were no lights in the cell, and it was very difficult to see me resting on my top slab. I was snuggled down in my rags when three guards from the group who had taken the law into their own hands passed my new cell, heading with rapid steps towards my old cell at the end of the hall.

Rome had extended herself. Then Jesus spoke to me and said, "Lie still." In a minute or so, I could hear the group coming back my way amid the gamblers. I could hear them saying, "Where did he go?" and looking in the cells, making an effort to find me.

The fierceness of the gamblers and my seeming disappearance worked a trip on their heads. Before they got to my cell, I heard the head guard say, "Let's get out of here." They passed my cell as fast as they had come, without looking in. The power of God was too heavy for them to stay. They had disfranchised themselves in a spiritual way by turning against the law God had given them. They couldn't stay amid my friends, the murderers.

A number of years before, while in the Air Force, I had spent a week in survival training on a small island in the Caribbean. I noticed that small fish fled in terror at the sighting of a shark. I was aware that some snakes and animals have a spiritual ability to bring their prey to a halt, making it very easy for them to take it. Spirits of terror and fear take up around natural animals to enable them to obtain food. Spirits also take up around men. I had experienced such strong spirits of terror from one killer that they rippled my flesh. The killers didn't bother me. I chuckled in my heart as their fierce spirits put the guards to route.

The new cell list had not been posted, and I had escaped. I wondered just what the guards had in mind doing. If they had wanted to beat on me some more, they would have come after lockdown. Everyone would have been locked up, and they ruled with little spiritual opposition at this time. I didn't know what was going on, so I decided I would not move as the fat man in Atlanta had. I was staying put.

A few days went by. I passed a friendly guard, and he said I was leaving that night. He was happy I was getting out. I walked to get my five-cent soda of the day, and someone else waved good-bye to me. Then there was a call for me to report to the clinic. Yea, I was leaving, but first I needed a medical. Big deal, big joke. I had been in the place for nearly three years, and I had never been given a medical. When a person left, he went out the front door. No medical, no nothing, gringo or Mexican—or so I understood.

The two doctors were grim and hard. These were not the two who told me they would protect me. They didn't want a medical; all they wanted was my name, rank, serial number, next of kin, scars, tattoos, or other body I.D. Who was my body going to be turned over to?

I got the drift of the exit. The doctors asked me about my family. As I talked about my family and my children, a very kind and sweet spirit of God came over me. I smiled and told the doctors I knew they were going to shoot me in Durango, but I told them I knew they had nothing to do with it. I smiled and was the happiest fellow one had ever seen. The joy of the Lord filled my soul. The two doctors looked at each other, and the one writing put down his pen. He called for a guard. He told the guard, "Sherman is in no state to be released. Send him back to his dorm."

I was so happy and full of joy of the Lord that I didn't even know what was going on.

The doctor who had given the order for me to be sent back was killed in a car accident shortly afterwards. I don't know what church he did or did not belong to, or even if he was saved. I do know that one day in Heaven I will see him again. Surely the passage in the Bible, *"Inasmuch as ye have done it unto one of the least of these my brethren, ye have done it unto me... enter in"*, applies here. *(Matthew 25:34-40)* I think he saved my life. This would pay for his ticket to heaven. Jesus was using situations to bring souls to a point of salvation.

A short time after this, I had a vision in my sleep, and Jesus spoke to me and told me I should get down to see the new Director as soon as possible that morning or a young man would be killed. I asked the guard on duty for permission to go to the main building to see the Director. Permission was granted, and passage through several gates was obtained.

As I passed the security officer's office, the rogue group was on duty. Sitting next to their office were two of the hardest and meanest men I had ever seen. I had to pass them on the way to the Director's office. As I approached them, one gave the other a jab with his elbow and said something, and four of the meanest eyes I had ever seen looked at me. They were fully armed. I passed them and entered the Director's office. I told him I repented of knocking over the statues and of all the trouble I had caused in the prison, and I wanted to pay for the damages. "Okay," he said, and I turned and left.

The two men were gone when I came back by the security officer's office. Later in the week, I saw their pictures in the newspaper. They were police officers and had been killed in a shoot out. In my mind I never was sure just who the young man was Jesus spoke of in the vision.

Statue bashing was not funny anymore. A lawyer had been appointed by the court to help me obtain a copy of the Veterans Administration medical report from Gainesville, Florida. He had a letter from the VA Hospital authorities saying the doctor who had filled out the medical report concerning me did work at the hospital. He also had a letter from the mayor of Gainesville, Florida saying the doctor in question resided in Gainesville and worked at the VA hospital.

He had talked to the judge, and the judge told him if I signed the papers I would be released in two weeks. I was certified to be insane; all I had to do now was to agree with them and sign my name and I was on the way out.

If I was insane, my signature was worthless. I told my lawyer I wasn't nuts and I wasn't signing. If they wanted to turn me loose then okay, but I was not touching the exit papers.

Long before this I had written the State Department of the United States of America and told them whoever honored the medical reports from the Veterans Administration Hospital in Gainesville, Florida, which were posted as a result of my visit there, whoever honored those reports which stated the language of God was babbling and called the praising of God a foolish or bazaar action, God's harsh judgment would fall upon them.

I would be insane to honor the reports. By honoring them, I would agree or say amen to them.

Some did honor them, and those who did ended up in some horrible tragedy. To some, the idea of me not wanting out after being given a way was insane. I knew better. When the door opened, I would leave—in God's time.

I wouldn't sign, and no one would touch the matter. Everyone hung tough. In God's Ordained Time I would leave.

There had always been a gap between me and the hard-core group of strong spirited men in the prison. After the beating and starving, I was now one of them. Rome had been retired with the bases loaded in the top of the ninth. It was the bottom of the ninth inning—the score tied, and the Jewish homerun hitter was coming up to bat in place of Sherman. This Fellow had a record of never failing to hit a homerun.

The new Director brought a change to the power structure in the prison. Some of the group of guards who had beat me left the prison, and those who stayed turned to Jesus. No charge had been laid! Towards my final days, these men became like guardian angels concerning my safety. The guard who held his fire with his mace can because of my warning was placed at nearly the top of his group. God blessed him. Jesus had moved on hearts, the last stronghold of bondage.

Jesus still hovered overhead with a great display of strength.

Chapter Eleven

Hang Him!

...that no flesh should glory in His presence...
1 Corinthians 1:29

Everyone had problems, so my presence and problems didn't bother anyone. There was still the unwritten law of silent war between the guards and inmates. I was now very much one of the inmates.

One night a man with a lean and hungry look cast his shadow at my cell door. He started a conversation, which was aimed at provoking the men around me. Why had I destroyed the statue of Jesus and knocked the head off the virgin downtown? A small crowd gathered, and people stood wanting answers. "We hang people like you here in Mexico as an example to other gringos," he said sarcastically, with a threatening overtone.

Eyes were starting to widen and open, and the group pressed against me and my cell bars. I was now facing a real live lynching mob. There was no way any inside or outside help could reach me in time if they decided to string me up.

"Alright, alright, you want answers? You'll get 'em." I had their attention. My Spanish was limited, but the words started coming out of my mouth. "First of all," I stuttered, "the statue that was pushed over downtown wasn't Mary. The doll didn't have black hair. Mary had black hair. Maybe it was someone else, but it wasn't Mary." O.K., they could buy this, but, "the statue on the cross? That was Jesus," someone said.

"Oh, no. The dude on the cross wasn't Jesus. Everyone knows Jesus didn't have any underwear when He hung on the cross. *(Matthew 27:35)* He was naked. The soldiers took everything He had. The statue had a sheet for underwear." They looked at one another with big eyes and nodded their heads. They knew this was true. They knew this by firsthand experience. They knew what the soldiers had done to them.

"Let me tell you the truth of the matter," I said. "That was a false Christ I shoved over. The soldiers took everything Jesus had and beat and killed him." *(Matthew 27)* The point was being driven home. The tension of the small group abated. Like a hard driving trial lawyer I pounded, "And you know who comes in the prison with the soldiers? The *Padre.* The *Padre* and the soldiers are in this thing together." That was all it took. I was found not guilty. The group broke up, and the fellow with the lean hungry look walked away. My advocate from the Most High Courts had given me the words to win my case. *(Matthew 10:19)*

~~~~~~~~~~~~~~~~~~

I decided it would be best to stay in my cell and

not go anywhere for a number of weeks. The aftermath of the false Christ bashing still hovered in parts of the 'joint'.

There was still the possibility that any misunderstood move on my part could bring down an instant judgment. The guards in the towers along the walls had big long rifles. I did not want to give them the opportunity for a few minutes of target practice, saying I had gone for the wall. Jesus backed me on my decision. The men I counted as my friends also gave me a silent agreement, and they would show up each day with sandwiches and coffee. I had much time to fast and pray.

One afternoon as I sat relaxing on my cement slab, a flickering light on the wall caught my attention. A vision started forming on the wall, as on a movie screen. The Stars and Stripes, the flag of the United States of America, my nation, appeared. The flag had a sparkling sheen covering it. I faintly heard the word, "leprosy." Then, to the right appeared the flames of hell. I watched as the flag of the United States sailed into the flames. It was gone into a fiery hell. Then, I heard the voice of a prophet say, "Ah, Lord, will you make an end of us all?" I saw a hand reach into the flames and pull out a remnant of the burnt flag with a few stars on it.

Then the vision was gone. Emotions welled up in my heart. No tears fell, but there was an inward weeping of God's Holy Spirit as I sat in silence before the fading vision. I had no inward leading concerning the time that the United States would be turned into the flames of hell, but it was my understanding a plague of leprosy came just before that time. I know other men have had visions of the coming doom of the United States. This was my vision. I can only speak for myself.

No nation can say it is a Christian nation. They may say this, but in truth, Jesus went to the Gentile nations of the world to call a people unto Himself. He did not single out any Gentile nations, but unto those nations where He had spiritual tribes, which found His pleasure, to these He gave good leaders and blessed them for His people's sake. The blessings went to the nations that sent out the most anointed Christian missionaries.

In one vision, Jesus let me see the spiritual blessing that was to come to Mexico in the coming years. The spiritual tribe of that nation had touched The Almighty, The Giver and Taker of all things, and found His pleasure. The blessings would come, little by little, over a period of time.

~~~~~~~~~~~~~~~~~

One morning, Rojo, a young man from northern Durango, sat at the volleyball court watching a game. Two of his 'friends' came up behind him and started to deliver punishing blows to Rojo's head with lead pipes. Down went Rojo, with a crushed skull. The men threw the pipes down and walked off. The alarms went off, and meekly they surrendered. Their defense was that Rojo had said he was going to kill them. They had gotten drunk on something that morning and decided they would get Rojo before he got them.

Rojo had gotten saved and started preaching. What he had said was that God was going to kill them if they didn't get right.

Through a miracle, Rojo was healed and soon returned from the hospital. He had a withered arm, but with his good arm he was an excellent marksman with a rifle. He was in prison for killing several members of a very large family in a shoot out. He also came from a very large family.

Many times, when men were released they would go back to face a vendetta in their villages. I gave Rojo a large Bible as he left upon his release from the prison. He waved good-bye and patted his Bible. "I have my Bible," he said. As he turned and walked towards the main office, I could see a horrible murder spirit take up a position over him. The prison had been his spiritual protector, but as he went away from the prison, the sins of his blood came home to roost. "Oh, Jesus," I prayed, "get him to a safe place." It wasn't long before Rojo strapped his guns on and was killed in a shoot out. His dad and a number of his brothers and kin strapped their guns on and headed to a fiesta, where they were sure they would find the members of the family who had killed Rojo.

The fiesta was in high gear as Rojo's dad and family lined along one side of the large building where it was being held. Someone made a move, and everyone dropped to the floor as the shooting began. When it was over, two or three members of each family were dead in pools of blood, and Rojo's dad and brothers were in jail.

How senseless. I am a fighter, make no mistake about that fact, but I fight in the will of God and with the spiritual power of God. This way Jesus gets all the credit. *(Zechariah 4:6)*

~~~~~~~~~~~~~~~~~~

Many eyes had watched the events that swirled around me. Not much was said, but I could spot the winning evidence of the effectiveness of the silent war that was being waged and won in the spirit. The prison had tamed down. Rather than curse me, some of the men would laugh and say, "Good time for you, Sherman." They had come to some godly knowledge. *(Psalm 140:8,9)* Shortly thereafter, a good time would come to them.

One day, as I passed the guard's office in our dorm, I was beckoned into the office by the guard on duty with a wave of his hand and, "Gringo, come here." A large Mexican guard whom I knew to be an honest and fair person sat before me. "I want you to give me one of those blocks of wood with that prayer you say," he said.

A lot of my time I would spend in prayer and meditation. During this time, I would take small blocks of soft, white pine, sand them smooth and imprint on them the 140th Psalm, verses eight and nine. I would oil them and pass them out.

That morning, I made three very good tablets. Going to dinner, I again passed the guard's office. He was waiting on me. I was a little surprised, as I didn't think the desire for the gringo's tablets would hold his attention throughout the morning. He waved me into the office. Where was his tablet? I quickly handed him one. "Sit down," he ordered. I sat down. He then took the smooth piece of wood with the Bible verses written on them, placed them on his table, and pulled his Spanish Bible from the drawer. He opened the Bible to the corresponding Psalm pressed in the wood. Word by word, he went over it, and without looking up, he said, "You can go."

This was a high point with my ministry. The guard sat fixed somewhat to the powerful verses of God's Word. I didn't matter as much as the words of strength, life and help he had before him. I had delivered my message and had gotten no glory. This had been my aim.

Chapter Twelve

The Last Mile

*And through a window in a basket was I let down by the
wall, and escaped his hands. 2 Corinthians 11:33*

The new Catholic priest was slowly working
his way down the hall, talking to the men as he
passed. He passed Sherman's cell and gave him a
respectful nod; Sherman, the gringo, the hated devil
who had destroyed the images in the prison and
without, a bane to the Catholic effort within the
prison. No doubt, the priest felt his faith was strong
enough to turn Sherman to righteousness, to bring
this gringo to a point of understanding the Catholic
way. It wasn't that Sherman didn't understand the
Catholic way; he knew it better than the priest. All
the death and hell the monster from Rome brought
upon the land, Sherman knew of it firsthand.

Then, by a leading of the Holy Spirit, Sherman
reached out to the priest in conversation, handed
him a small Gideon Bible in Portuguese and said,
"Sir, I want you to know this prison is my church
and you are welcome to come and go."

The words were not spoken without purpose. I
felt my time was over in the prison. In effect, I was
handing the matter of spiritual authority back to the
people I had so boldly taken it from. Spiritual
matters had greatly changed, both within the walls

of the prison I called home and outside in the city of Durango. I knew thousands upon thousands of people had prayed for not only me, but for Mexico and its people during the many months I had been in the prison. Several times the door had been opened for me to leave, but each time Jesus had encouraged me to stay.

I had come to Mexico to tell people about the saving grace of Jesus and His ever-present help to a person in need. This Great Spirit God is present at all times and is able to give help to all when called upon. *(Matthew 28:20)* I was not a member of any church or denomination, nor was I ordained by any man or organization. I just had a burning, fervent desire to tell everyone I could about Jesus and how He had helped me.

One time, as the door opened for me to leave, I walked out to the prison yard and saw all the young men playing baseball and working on various projects. The Scripture about King Asa's conduct regarding the statues and images of his time came to mind. *(2 Chronicles 14:2-4)* He overthrew them, and then he taught his people the law and commandment of God. For sure, I had thrown over the idols and disrupted the spiritual life of Durango. I had not run, and as I gazed across the yard this morning, I felt it was not time to leave; the law and commandment of God had to be taught.

This had been some time back. Now, I felt the

situation had reached a place where the Mexicans, who watched over me without yielding to the tremendous outside pressures that called for my blood, could stand no more. My time was drawing to an end.

I was standing in the prison yard one morning talking to several Americans. We were approached by a Drug Enforcement Agency Agent from the United States. He was a Mexican-American from Los Angeles, California. From time to time, he would make a visit to the prison to pick what information he could from the Americans there.

This was the first time I had met him, and I was dressed in my Sunday best rags. He took one look at me, and then cut his eyes in a thoughtful glance. "Oh, no," he said, "Sherman ain't crazy." The Mexicans never did understand me, but this guy was as street smart as they come, and he picked up my act right away, if I did have an act. When David was captured, he caused his captors to think he was insane and found a way out in this manner. *(1 Samuel 21:13-15)* It didn't bother me if I was considered insane by the authorities. There was nothing I could do to convince them otherwise anyway.

There was somewhat of a division between the United States Central Intelligence Agency and the Drug Enforcement Agency concerning how to deal with the drug smugglers from the United States. One newspaper had reported that the DEA wanted to declare war on the smugglers and wipe them out, but the CIA wanted to use them to obtain information, as they went into strange places and knew a lot about the power structure of these areas. I don't know what the outcome of this situation was, but I felt the guy from Los Angeles must have told the Mexican authorities that the CIA did strange things, and somehow I must be connected with them. I couldn't get away from the CIA and all its mystery.

The Cuban who drove the Director's car must have had some link with the Cuban intelligence system. The war in Vietnam had come to a close, but the KGB, CIA, and other intelligence agencies still worked around the clock doing all things to maintain the control of the world powers.

I was well aware that the KGB had all the records of the United States officers, Army, Navy, Air Force, or whatever. They had the goods on computers. One can only guess how they got them. The Director of the prison was the nephew of the President of Mexico and had access to intelligence information. One day our friendly relationship turned into a frosty morning. I pondered the freeze until one of the guards told me that the Director had told them I was with the CIA.

My past had gone before me. True, I had been distantly associated with the CIA and a U-2 spy plane operation while a pilot in the United States Air Force. I had helped fly rescue aircraft for the lonely highflying U-2's. All our work was done in the Western Hemisphere sampling the atmosphere for radioactive fallout, and I had played only a small innocent role.

The sin of the CIA had overshadowed me, but my God is great, and somehow we would get over the bump. Jesus and I would get over it. The Director now wanted me out of the prison. The Catholics in town wanted me out of the prison, and I am sure the new priest wanted me out. In his mind, I was beyond hope—a crazy gringo.

I had been sentenced to six years for damaging government property and preaching in the streets of Durango. All the churches in Mexico belonged to the government, so they had no problem getting me to agree that I was indeed a criminal of sorts. Three years and a month or so of my sentence had passed. I had no working time towards release. My case had become a political hot potato and no one would touch it, including myself.

The only way I was going to get out of the Durango State Prison was by the authorities opening the front gate and telling me to leave, as ordered by the Lord of all, Jesus Christ. I felt giving the spiritual authority back to the priest was the first step in this direction. Others would follow.

Shortly after my conversation with the visiting Catholic priest, the Lord visited me with prophetic knowledge of the date I would leave the prison. *(Acts 27:23,24)* Later in the morning I was walking in the prison yard, my Bible in hand, writing in it the date when I would leave the prison. 'Big John', a drug dealer from Hartford, Connecticut, passed me by. "Hey, whatcha doing?" he said.

"I am writing down the date upon which I shall walk through the gates of this city and become a free man."

"Yeah, I bet," laughed John.

"Okay, we'll see," I said.

John was a newcomer to the prison in Durango. He had spent time in prison in Juarez and elsewhere. There was something that God liked about John. His claim to fame was that he had moved a ton of marijuana across the Mexican-United States border right under the nose of the customs officers.

John said that after all the drugs he had done he was having trouble with his mind. Out of the Sierra Madres he had come, with a bundle of marijuana under his car hood. He said one Hail Mary after the other, and things only got worse. He said he then thought he would try the Lord's Prayer. As soon as the words 'Thy will be done' were said, he turned the corner and there stood two federal police.

"Hey man, these dudes were straight as they come—they popped the hood of my car and found my bundle. I tried to give them money, anything, but all they said was, 'Fellow, you're coming with us.'" Big John knew what was coming next. He had a single, one-hundred-dollar bill.

The police took everything else he had, but John had made up his mind he was going to hold on to his hundred-dollar bill. He swallowed it, and a day or two later he swallowed it again, and a day or two later when John entered the prison, he brought with him his well-digested one hundred dollar bill. Old Ben had traveled an acidy, rough road. John didn't lose his hundred-dollar bill, but a few days later he lost his bet with me.

~~~~~~~~~~~~~~~~~

Tony was one of the assistant directors in the prison. He was short and well built, with a flat top haircut. On occasions he would wear his military uniform. He looked sharp with his tall, high laced jump boots and small pair of silver wings pinned on his military shirt. Tony ran his shift by the book. He spent some of his childhood in California and could speak pretty good English. Most of my dealings with authorities were with Tony.

We got to know each other pretty good, and I think we developed a bit of respect for each other, if this was possible under the circumstances.

He did not want me loose in the main yard. He was pretty adamant about this, as he felt I would be harmed or killed. If he had his way, I would have been ushered out the front door. Tony did fear God, but if you were talking for God you had better be mighty right. He was Catholic but said he didn't pay much attention to what was said or went on in the church.

As time progressed, he became involved in the subject of religion and just what was going on concerning the gringo and the prison.

The coffee shop was the free zone in the prison. The inmates ran it, and you could get a cup of coffee or a sandwich and not be involved in the prison system. I spent a good bit of time there.

One day, I asked for a very hot cup of coffee. The large wood burner took its time about warming things up. A new man, Poncho, was helping behind the counter. Poncho's sin was homosexuality, and he had a pretty bold case of it.

For Poncho, being in prison was like a fox in the hen house. He flirted like a woman, and I guess you could say he was gay. Whatever, I didn't appreciate him knocking my spoon every time I tried to dip a spoonful of sugar out of the bowl.

I told him in no uncertain terms to stop and leave me alone. Somehow my coffee cup became the focal point of a small struggle. I was at my wits' end about being shoved around. I held my coffee up and told him to back off, or I was going to throw the coffee on him. With boldness, he grabbed at my hand and gave my cup a good shove. The black stuff went on my beard but didn't scald me.

The hot coffee in my beard was too much, and something in my head snapped. I tried to throw the coffee in his face, but a great weight came over my arm and all I could do was toss the very hot coffee down his shirt. Jesus had come upon the scene.

Poncho let out some squeaks and some other strange noises and danced a jig around the big wood-burning stove.

Talk about strange things happening! Jesus burst into the room in a ball of fire. When this ball of fire appeared, I was scared. Jesus made a slow circle in the coffeehouse, and such anger I have never seen so expressed on a man before. It was as if He dared anyone to even touch me. I was scared, but seeing the Master back my actions with such a dramatic supernatural display of protection heartened me greatly.

Poncho hit the door running, and I sat down. I knew what was coming next. Several minutes later, a tall guard stuck his head in the door and said, "Come with me." I was 'under arrest' and locked up. I was so very sorry about what had happened, but what was done was done.

Poncho was something else. That afternoon he made a pass at some guy in the showers, and the guy decked him. He now sported a big black eye and a red *sunburn* on the chest.

I didn't sleep much that night. The next day the Catholic newspapers grabbed the news, and in bold headlines the story was told of how I had scalded this poor boy and what a grave physical condition he was in. The Catholic newspaper knew one thing for sure; their man Anthony (Tony) was going to see to it that the gringo got his due, and they printed it as such.

The next morning, very early, I was escorted to Tony's office to have '*my say*'. Poncho was sitting on one side of the room. He had '*his say*'. I wasn't able to catch what '*his say*' was.

Then Tony turned to me and asked what happened. I said, "I don't guess it matters, as no one would believe me anyway."

Then Tony said something that touched my heart. "Yes, they will, I will believe you." I didn't know who hit Poncho, and later I was to get the blame, but this morning little Tony rose up like a true lion. Tony didn't scare; he knew the Catholics were pushing him, and he didn't like it.

You didn't push Tony, and he was running his shift by the book. Not only did Tony not like the idea of his authority being pushed, but he also didn't like Poncho. I don't know what the Mexican prison policy on homosexuals is today, but when I was there, they were segregated and warned to 'get real' or get put in the inner prison.

I told Tony the short story of the coffee tossing. He said, "Okay," he believed me, but it wasn't a good idea for me to be in the main prison. He didn't know what to do about it.

My one night stay 'jail' was over.

One guard asked me, "Why did you scald Poncho?" I told him it was much better to burn here, rather than burn in hell. He laughed and said, "The punishments of God." When I left the prison, Poncho had come a long way toward getting the thing right; you bet I prayed a lot for him.

From time to time, Tony would turn his ear to what I had to say. One day he showed up at the door of the small grocery store they had in the prison. Sodas were a nickel. Big, tall ones. Tony was smiling and wanted to talk religion. A small gold chain with a medal of some Catholic saint dangled around his neck. He pulled it out and proceeded to tell me and those listening that Mary was the mother of us all, and we can say prayers to her. *Hey, this is a new role for tough Tony,* I thought.

Behind me a few men gathered, and someone laughed and said, "Yea, Sherman, that's the statue you beat up with a hammer."

I quickly told everyone, "I didn't beat the doll with a hammer, my hand shoved it over." My words came out so quick, flat, and honest, that Tony knew what I said was true.

A funny look came over his face as he realized someone at the church must have beaten the head off the doll. Tony had been around the block several times and had seen and heard it all. Maybe one or two days out of the year you could con him, but Tony was no man's fool. I had no reason to lie.

To no one present was the hammer or what I had to say in question, except to Tony, and in his mind, he figured that maybe someone else should be in the prison for damaging government property.

Tony left without saying much more. Later, after the false Christ bashing, very strong pressures were brought against him to do something to the gringo.

He stood his ground, and I am sure it cost him favor in political places, but I am also sure he gained favor at "the top" where it counted. Jesus wrote it all down, and on the final day when it counts, Tony will have a "Friend" on his side—and what a Friend is Jesus.

Somehow, we obtained a copy of a revolutionary newspaper. It told the story of how a young man had been killed in the prison, and the blame was put on Tony. He was pretty much vilified, and the article was an open request for someone to shoot Tony.

Tony needed help. I worked hard on a wooden tablet with the 140th Psalm, verses 8 and 9, pressed in the soft wood. I then asked to see Tony. I was escorted into his office. I handed him the tablet and said, "I want to give this to you."

He looked at it and said, "Thanks." He seemed to appreciate the prayer and appeared to have a generous spirit towards me. He then said, "Is this all, do you want anything?"

"No," I replied. This was a new twist. He

hadn't seen this act come across his desk before, but he bought it.

Tony weathered the matter and became a very strong tower of truth. People were taking sides and being sealed towards that final and terrible Day of Judgment.

I was in the carpenter shop working when Tony came by, escorting the two men through the prison whom I felt had come to take me to the border the next day.

He passed me and could hardly contain the news that I was leaving. He didn't say anything, but by his manner, he tried to convey to me what I already knew. It didn't matter, as Jesus had given me the news a few days before.

I am sure the report Tony gave the two men concerning my stay in the prison enabled them to show me the great favor they would display towards me in Nuevo Laredo two days later.

Later in the day, the two men who were with Tony in the carpenter shop happened to pass by my cell with the Assistant Director. We chatted a moment or two, and I showed them the tablets with Bible verses I was working on. I gathered from the manner of respect shown them that they were from a high level in the government. The Lord then spoke to me and told me I would be leaving with these two men.

The morning of the prophetic date I had written in my Bible was off to a slow start, but soon came the call for Sherman to report to the main prison office to see the Director. I entered the Director's office, and he told me I was being released that afternoon. I thanked him and left.

I gave away nearly everything I had, as a group of men gathered at my cell. I kept the rags I had on, a small box full of prayer cloths, and a bottle of oil. Two guards came to usher me to the main office. As we passed the entrance to the area where the Americans were stored, a group of them were standing at the gate yelling, "Hey, the prophecy came true! You are leaving!" Praise God, I was on my way out.

The American drug dealers were hard, and only John had turned to my message of Jesus Christ, yet here they were acting like a bunch of kids who had just won the state basketball championship. I knew they would be in for a rough time after I left. I said, "Look, why don't you guys give your lives to the Lord Jesus before I go? He'll protect you and see you get out okay." Big John snorted and said, "Why not," and all the gringos present got down on their knees and accepted Jesus. I was then escorted to the main office.

Here, I was told to sign some papers and I would be released with the two men I had seen the day before, and escorted the border. A lot of papers were shoved at me. My Spanish was very limited, and in no way could I read and understand what the papers said. I said, "I'm not signing anything." For many months, I had refused to sign papers. I wasn't going to put my John Henry on a lot of stuff I didn't know beans about.

Hands flew up in the air, and indignation rolled around the room. "You're not going to sign?"

I said, "No, I'm not going to sign."

"You can't get out of prison unless you sign."

Again, I said I would not sign. I did not know what would happen next, but God Almighty had said I was leaving today, and if God Almighty Who caused the sun to come up and the sun to go down said I was leaving, then they could wave all their hands in the air and look hard and bug-eyed and mean at me all they wanted to. I didn't care, because Jesus had His hand on the entire exit.

The headman of the two men waiting to escort me to the border reached across the desk, grabbed the papers, and barked, "I'll sign it! Let's get the show on the road!"

No one protested, and everyone was glad the signing was over. This wasn't MacArthur and Tokyo Bay, but it meant as much to me. Then the agent who had just signed my walking papers said, "Let's go." It was a great moment for me, and I shook hands with many of the guards as they saw me off.

For sure, all these wonderful Mexicans had come from God. I felt I had been lowered over the wall in a basket as we were given a first class ride to the bus station.

Mexico moves on its bus system, clean and safe. We picked up our tickets, boarded the waiting bus, and settled into the plush seats for the long ride to the border. So far, the *escape* had been uneventful. We rode all night. I didn't get any sleep and prayed all the way. Dawn came slowly as we pushed into Nuevo Laredo on the Mexican-United States border. Here I had to pass through the Mexican Customs and Immigration before going across the border.

We entered the large building that housed the Mexican Customs and Immigration offices. Here again, I sat before more armed men with pencils and papers and was told to sign. The two men who had escorted me this far looked on, and no one smiled. Again, many pages of Spanish that I had no way of understanding were being shoved at me. Again, I said, "I'm not signing them."

On the bus, I had shown the two Mexican agents the scripture in the Bible where Jesus says to *'let your yea be yea; and your nay, nay'* and *'swear not' (James 5:12, Matthew 5:34,37)* This was the reason I would not sign at the prison in Durango. The Word of God seemed to satisfy them at the time. All the way on the bus to Nuevo Laredo, I had wondered if they had guns. I tried to see any sign of guns strapped to them as they moved about, but I never saw anything. They were dressed in plain pants and shirts with green windbreaker jackets.

A large Mexican Customs officer shook his fist in my face and replied, "You'll go to prison here in Nuevo Laredo if you don't sign." Here again, the two little men of action and authority made their move. The next thing I knew, the mild man of action and authority had a black snub-nosed pistol stuck in the face of the Mexican Customs official who had just stuck his fist in my face. It was gangbusters and Brooklyn winning the series against the Yanks all over again.

I'm sitting at this table, and I can hear the Rio Grande River running under the window behind me. Only a few feet to freedom across the small stream that served to separate two nations, yet as far as I was concerned it could have been a hundred miles wide. *I've come so far through so much, and now I'm going to get shot in a shoot out at the last minute.* Then the words of Jesus came to me: "Oh ye of little faith."

I wasn't praying. I wasn't thinking. I was just watching. The man of authority's buddy backed into the office entrance and covered the room with his small, black, snub-nosed pistol. He had one also. He had the drop on everyone as this wonderful little Mexican stuck his I.D. card in the customs officer's face and said he had orders to get me safely to the United States. The little agent's eyes narrowed and his nostrils flared, and he waved his small pistol while he talked.

"Give me your Bible," the small man

commanded. He extended his hand towards me, never turning his head or lowering his pistol. "Show me the place in the Bible you pointed out to me earlier." Time seemed to stand still, and my fingers all felt like thumbs. Somehow, I managed to find Matthew 5 very fast.

The other customs officials stood against the walls of the room with their hands in the air, and everyone listened as the little agent read from my Bible why I didn't have to sign, "Swear not." *(Matthew 5:33,37)* I sat in awe and heard the greatest sermon I had ever heard preached; "He doesn't have to sign! He is a man of God, and he is going across the border!"

I thought after the small agent had made his point he might put his pistol away. He didn't! Both of the agents kept the room covered with their pistols. They backed out the door of the office and blocked the sidewalk that led back into Mexico. I was sure glad to have them on my side, or to be on their side, but the two pistols did make me a bit nervous.

The two little men were real pros at their profession. They knew just who they were and what awesome authority they had. They had been given orders, and they were not going to discuss or argue the point. They were well prepared to shoot first, then ask or answer any questions.

The large Mexican Customs officer who had shaken his fist in my face agreed at once that I did not have to sign and was free to go. I shook the hands of the two men who spoke for the nation of Mexico. At the last minute, at the last mile, a Mexican office received me as a man of God. Everyone seemed dazed and staggered from the shock of the small black pistols and such high authority. As I shook their hands, I spoke from an even higher authority, "Thank you and God bless you." Then I headed for the bridge. Halfway across the international bridge, my sandals broke, and I tossed them into the Rio Grande.

Barefooted, in rags, with twenty-eight cents and my vegetable crate with the prayer cloths and a small bottle of oil, I crossed the bridge over the Rio Grande River, the border line between the United States of America and the Republic of Mexico, and entered the United States at Laredo, Texas. It was very early in the morning, and my stay in Mexico had just ended with a silent spiritual thunderclap. I was now in another world. A tall Texan dressed in Border Patrol Green greeted me as I passed through the United States Customs.

"Are you a citizen of the United States?"

"Yes," I answered.

"Where have you been and where are you coming from?"

I answered that I was coming from Durango, Mexico, where I had been in prison. "Hm, well..." He stood looking at me, and his mind was trying to put my situation all together. The officer then asked, "Do you have an I.D.?"

I told him, "No."

"What were you in prison for?" he questioned farther.

I told him, "Preaching."

The whole matter was something new to a man who I am sure had seen it all pass his station. "OK," he said. He took a deep breath, then let out a deep, "Whew! Where are you going?"

I said, "I am going to a revival."

This was too much to go into anymore at this early hour. He rolled his eyes in his head and said, "I guess so, go on." And through the gates into a new prison I passed, but I still had the freedom of my soul in Jesus Christ.

Where I would go I didn't know, but my ever-present help would surely guide and provide for me—Jehovah Jireh, The Lord, My Provider. *(Genesis 22:14)*

Epilogue

Sherman walked through Laredo, Texas barefooted in the early hours of the morning. At a grocery store on the edge of town, he bought twenty-three cents worth of hamburger and ate it raw. No bun, just raw beef. The look he received from the store manager was louder than words. "Get out of my store, you bum!" said 'the look'.

He then came to the Houston highway, and with the leading of the Lord he headed for Houston, Texas hitchhiking. The rides were all ordained of God. He was given a pair of good sandals in one town before arriving in Houston.

Sherman arrived that night at the home of Christian friends in Houston. He was greeted with nearly the same words and manner that Peter received when he walked out of the prison in Jerusalem and arrived at the home of Mary. These charitable people made it possible for him to have a suit of clothes and the airfare to Atlanta, Georgia. After several days of rest, prayer, and fellowship, Sherman departed on a night flight for Atlanta, Georgia.

It was midnight when Sherman arrived at the Atlanta Airport. From the front door of the airport terminal, he started hitch hiking to Cleveland, Tennessee. Rides were ready and waiting as ordered by the Lord, and early the following morning, Sherman arrived to be with the group that had stood so faithfully with him while he was in Mexico. The curtain came down on the final act of the prophecy of the Lord.

He sat and told the group of all the trials, temptations, and wonders of God he had faced while in Mexico. The tall slender Man of God had been correct in his prophecy.

About the author

Roberto Sherman Gunnels was born in Brunswick, Georgia on the 1st day of January in 1932. The Almighty, Jesus Christ, revealed Himself to Brother Sherman on April the 6th in 1966 and called him into a spiritual ministry. There isn't much noteworthy to say about Brother Sherman before this time. After Brother Sherman's revelation of the Truth there isn't much noteworthy to say about him, except he does know the Lord Jesus Christ, and this is very noteworthy.

Brother Sherman still stands on street corners and visits the marketplaces with signs painted on his jacket and car, warning the passerby of the soon coming of Jesus Christ and to prepare to flee the wrath of God. He keeps it very simple. He belongs to no organized church, nor does he have any ordainment papers issued by man. He says he has a book full of papers in God's Word.

Brother Sherman looks forward to that day when he walks the last mile in his life—at the final minute on the banks of that final river, no other desire does he have except to be surrounded by a band of Holy Angels of the Lord Jesus Christ, to see their drawn shining swords at the ready, and to hear their leader say, "He's a man of God and we have orders from the King of Kings to see that he gets safely across." And sir, this will be worth it all.